LAUNCH YOUR DIVORCE WORKBOOK

by Wanda Bailey

Step-by-Step Guide from Start to Finish

www.dragongempublishing.com

LAUNCH YOUR DIVORCE WORKBOOK

Published by Dragon Gem Publishing
Copyright © 2017 by Wanda Bailey
Cover by Wanda Bailey

All rights reserved. No part of this publication may be reproduced, stored, or transmitted in any form or by any means, electronic, mechanical, photocopying, recording, scanning, or otherwise, except as permitted under Section 107 or 108 of the 1976 United States Copyright Act, without the prior written permission of the author. Requests to the author and publisher for permission should be addressed to the following email: wanda@dragongempublishing.com

Limit of liability/disclaimer of warranty: While the publisher and author have used their best efforts in preparing this guide, checklists and spreadsheet, they make no representations or warranties with respect to the accuracy or completeness of the contents of this document and specifically disclaim any implied warranties of merchantability or fitness for particular purpose. No warranty may be created or extended by sales representatives, promoters, or written sales materials.

The advice and strategies contained herein may not be suitable for your situation. You should consult with a professional where appropriate. Neither the publisher nor author shall be liable for any loss of profit or any other commercial damages, including but not limited to special, incidental, consequential, or other damages.

Note – Much of the content of this workbook was previously published in the book Divorce Blueprint (2015). This edition has additional content and workbook pages not previously published.

P.S. Some of the resources contained herein are affiliate links, meaning that at no extra cost to you, I may make a commission if you decide to purchase one of the mentioned items. I thank you for supporting me, my family, and our dreams.

Also by Wanda Bailey

Divorce Blueprint (2015)

Weight Loss Back 2 Basics (2015)

Going Gluten Free (2015)

Fortune – A Journal for Oracle and Tarot Card Readings (2016)

Dedication

This book is dedicated to all of the folks that are leaving a relationship that somehow went bad. Whether you are leaving, or your partner is leaving – it really sucks. In time, may you experience hope for the future, and peace.

And please don't smack talk about your partner. You're better than that.

Contents

Dedication – 4

Preface - 7

About the Author – 9

01 - Do you REALLY want to break up / divorce? - 13

02 - Pre-Divorce Checklist - 25

03 - Legal Matters - 27

04 - Creating Your Divorce Plan – 35

05 – What to Say to Friends, Family, Employers - 39

06 - Where Will You Live? - 41

07 - Helping Children Cope - 45

08 - During the Divorce Checklist - 49

09 – Budgeting - 53

10 - Dividing Assets & Debts - 96

11 - Military Divorce - 71

12 - Divorcing a Passive Aggressive Partner - 79

13 – Divorcing a Narcissistic Partner – 85

14 – When the Crazy Goes down - 87

15 - Miss Manners - 95

16 - Things I Wish I'd Known - 99

17 - After the Divorce Checklist - 105

Closing Remarks - 109

Appendix A - The Divorce Playlist – 111

Appendix B – Make Your Own Calendar - 115

Preface

"Divorce isn't such a tragedy. A tragedy's staying in an unhappy marriage, teaching your children the wrong things about love. Nobody ever died of divorce."

~ Jennifer Weiner, Fly Away Home

How Launch Your Divorce came to be…

I was miserable. I'd been a bad marriage for far too long. We'd tried counseling, multiple times – and we'd stick with our "agreements" for four to six months, and then we'd backslide. We were destructive to each other, all of our behaviors concentrating on wounding our partner to make up for real or imagined slights.

I stayed, we stayed together – at first, for financial reasons. At one point, I asked my parents for money for a divorce, and they didn't have any to give me. So I stayed. Later, we were bound together by kids, and financial hardship.

As the years went on, I finally felt financially comfortable enough to make the break – and what I did, and how I did it, are what you'll find laid out in this book.

You, dear reader – may be in a similar boat. Or worse – you may have had the subject of divorce sprung on you, and it's the last thing in the world that you want for yourself, and possibly your children. But fighting it is like fighting to stay on a sinking ship. It's going down, and you're not going to stop it.

You CAN take control of the process – by planning and preparing, and following through. It's not hard – sit down, get some paper, get your smart phone, get a calendar, make your plan. Read through the checklists and information included here. There are some additional resources sprinkled throughout this book, including:

- Checklists for Before, During, and After the Divorce Process
- Books to buy from your local bookstore or off of Amazon
- Other Information products to help with your Divorce, Parenting, and Recovery process
- Assets & Debts Spreadsheet (available from www.dragongempublishing/doingdivorcebetter)

Please keep reading – and don't feel like you need to read the entire workbook. You may just want to read it in parts – and that's okay. Divorce is difficult, no need to be overwhelmed all at once.

About the Author

Wanda Bailey has spoken to audiences on various topics and themes for thirty years, and created training programs for that long, as well! She's had many blessings in her life - she's worked in accounting and payroll, she's been a music director at two different churches. She's worked in staffing, web design and marketing, and was also a nanny!

She's traveled all over the United States of America doing software training, both in person, remotely, and in video presentations. She studied in Mexico as a teenager, and has visited Canada, Ireland, Germany and Austria.

She has four children - the youngest is almost finished with high school.

Q – So why do you think you're an expert on divorce?

A - My expertise on divorce has been a long time in the making! I observed my parents' divorce around 24 years ago, observed friends and family in divorces and relationship breakups – and then I experienced my own divorce.

I am a very curious person, and spent a lot of time looking up legal information about divorcing, finding out processes and procedures, and was asked by my attorney to research writing some software for divorce and family law attorneys. That did not end up panning out, but I kept all of the research, and have expanded on it over the last few years to the point that I was ready to share my findings – so here we are!

Wherever you are in the divorce process, there are things you need to do, think about, or be aware of. Inside this book are sections with lots of information broken up into smaller pieces – you can read the book in the order presented, or pick sections that apply to you, and skip ahead to learn more about the process that are pertinent to your situation. I've purposefully tried to keep everything gender-neutral, and some topics or information may not always be relevant to you. Whether you are in a legally binding marriage or a civil union, or just breaking up with a long-term partner, there's stuff you have to do and think about.

I'll be using the word "divorce" to cover all types of breakups.

I'll be using the word "attorney" to refer to a legal professional, which would include a solicitor, barrister, counselor, paralegal, scrivener, or a clerk to file papers.

A side note – **this is not a legal guide**. I'm not an attorney. I don't even play one on TV. This course is meant to guide you through the process OUTSIDE of the legalities, but keeping those legalities in mind. When I wanted a divorce – I spent a couple of months researching everything, makings lists, deciding how I wanted things to happen – in other words, I created a blueprint, if you will, for de-constructing my marriage.

The results – yes, I got divorced. And while it was painful, and heart-rending, and tore my family apart in many ways – it really wasn't so bad.

One of the things I want to make sure that you DON'T miss are the resources. I've put together some information throughout the book, including checklists, book recommendations, and even a Playlist for your divorce. I know – I'm a little crazy, but who doesn't like a little music to either cry their eyes out about, get mad about, or get all empowered about? And there's music crossing about 60 years, so there's something for everyone there. Check the back of this book for the playlist.

If you really do want a divorce – you have to work for it. Just because you say "I want a divorce" and see a lawyer – it's not going to automatically roll out. You have to keep on top of your attorney, and understand all of the deadlines and timeframes. In some regions, a divorce can go fairly quickly, as in a few weeks. But in many areas, there are waiting periods to be observed. These may be weeks, months, or years. If you really want a divorce, you have to stay on top of the rules and regulations governing the divorce, or you may have to start some waiting periods over again.

Legalese! Disclaimer!

This is not a legal textbook. I am not an attorney. Nor am I a psychiatrist or psychologist. I've been divorced for several years now, and a lot of this presentation is information I discovered before, during, and after my own divorce. ALWAYS ALWAYS ALWAYS consult an attorney or solicitor, whatever your call legal assistance in your part of the world, and seek professional counseling if you're having a rough time. Seriously. Yes, there are some bad attorneys, and bad counselors. But there are some really good ones, find one.

Alright then, let's get started!

"It's never too late to be who you might have been."

~ George Eliot

CHAPTER ONE

Do you REALLY want to break up / divorce?

Sometimes relationships hit a rocky patch. Rocky patches are a part of life's path through this world, and usually, you can keep on walking past the rocky parts, or find a better path. Having disagreements with your partner is normal, and part of a healthy and functioning relationship.

Following are some pointed questions to read through, and think about, as you contemplate your break-up. They may bring you to the point where you think - wow, none of this applies to me. If this is your situation, you may be taking things a little too far with your disagreements. Counseling is a very viable option and can help relationships last - or at least make them last a bit longer. I, myself, worked through counseling right after I married, and again before I divorced, in an attempt to save, or at least prolong my marriage.

If many of the questions apply to you - you've got some serious issues. Counseling might help you, if both you and your partner are committed to working out your issues. It takes two to tango! Don't let anyone tell you that marriage is a 50/50 partnership. ***It has to be 100% on both sides***, if it is to survive, and thrive. The periods in my marriage when we both worked hard on the relationship were the best years ever, and were some very happy times for both of us. But when one of us coasted – that's when problems take root and grow. If you've been the worker in the marriage, and someone else has been the coaster, you will have a lot of anger that your partner doesn't seem to care about. If you've been coasting, and your partner has asked you for a divorce, you may be stunned, and disoriented – you may have thought that since you provided well or cared for your household and the children, that's all you had to do. But you may have neglected your partner's needs, because you really did not take the time to know them! Let's go through some thoughtful questions to get our heads in the right place about the divorce. There are no right or wrong answers – but you may start to see patterns in your relationship that were fuzzy in the past, but become much clearer as you think about them.

The "Do I Really Want A Divorce" Quiz – use a pen or pencil as you work through these questions. Please feel free to write out questions or observations!

Do you love your partner?

    a) Yes

    b) No

_____

_____

_____

Does your partner love you?

    a) Yes

    b) No

_____

_____

_____

Does your partner make you feel good about yourself?

    a) Yes

    b) No

_____

_____

_____

Do you feel physically safe around your partner?

    a) Yes

    b) No

_____

_____

_____

Does your partner disrespect or degrade you?

    a) No

    b) Yes

_____

_____

_____

Has your partner cheated on you?

    a) No

    b) Yes

    c) I'm not sure

_____

_____

_____

If your partner HAS cheated on you, have you forgiven your partner?

    a) Yes

    b) No

    c) I'm working on it

_____

_____

_____

If your partner has cheated, has your partner's cheating behavior stopped?

    a) Yes

    b) No

    c) I don't know

_____

_____

_____

Have you cheated on your partner?

    a) No

    b) Yes

    c) Not exactly

_____

_____

_____

If so has your partner forgiven you?

    a) Yes

    b) No

    c) Not exactly

_____

_____

_____

Has your cheating behavior stopped?

    a) Yes

    b) No

    c) Not exactly

_____

_____

_____

Is your partner hiding financial dealings from you, or making purchases and hiding them? This is sometimes called financial infidelity.

    a) No

    b) Yes

    c) I don't know

_____

_____

_____

Are you hiding financial dealings from your partner, or making purchases and hiding them?

    a) No

    b) Yes

    c) Not exactly

_____

_____

_____

Does arguing with your partner negatively affect your child?

    a) No

    b) Yes

_____

_____

_____

Is your partner a threat to your child?

    a) No

    b) Yes

    c) Not exactly

_____

_____

_____

Do you hate or despise your partner?

    a) No

    b) Yes

    c) Not exactly

_____

_____

_____

Does your partner hate or despise you?

    a) No

    b) Yes

    c) I don't know

_____

_____

_____

Do you ever have thoughts of harming your partner to escape the relationship?

    a) No

    b) Yes

    c) Not exactly

_____

_____

_____

Does your partner physically harm you, or your child?

    a) No

    b) Yes

    c) Not exactly

_____

_____

_____

Do you physically harm your partner or your child?

    a) No

    b) Yes

    c) Not exactly

_____

_____

_____

Do you have thoughts about harming yourself to escape your partner?

    a) No

    b) Yes

    c) Not exactly

_____

_____

_____

Are you happier when your partner is not around?

    a) No

    b) Yes

    c) Not exactly

___

___

___

Are you physically attracted to your partner?

    a) Yes

    b) No

    c) Not exactly

___

___

___

Is your partner physically attracted to you?

    a) Yes

    b) No

    c) I don't know

___

___

___

Whew, you made it through the whole list! How do you feel? Do you feel better about your relationship? Do you feel the same? Do you feel worse? These questions cover a wide field of reasons for breaking up. If some of the questions disturbed you, or hit home - this can help you evaluate your decision to break up - or stay with your partner. You may have noticed a pattern in the answers – and rightly so.

The A) answers are positive answers. If you answered mostly A's - you're doing pretty well in your relationship. If your partner can't answer the same way - you guys need some maintenance work. Go see a counselor, and commit to a once-a-week maintenance session to review things before they start festering and driving one or the other of you crazy. You guys have a good chance of making this work.

The B) answers are negative answers - you guys are toast. Get a lawyer, and get out.

The C) answers are somewhat ambivalent – meaning that you are on the fence about the questions, or you're not really sure. This means that you, or your partner (or both), have been skating for a while, about your entire relationship. And you don't really care enough to make a change to fix it. If you're okay with this - you may just keep on chugging along for the rest of your lives, miserable with each other, finding happiness in other areas of your life. Many couples do this quite successfully. I find it pretty sad – but I did it, myself, for a long time.

If you're still undecided, you may want to stop and review this section twice, or even a third time. Divorce isn't something that you make a decision about quickly – there are a lot of things to evaluate. I wouldn't wish divorce on anyone – but on the other hand, I don't wish endless misery – or endless nothing-ness. Does your partner fulfill you spiritually? If you were both to die tomorrow, would you hold hands as you faced your religious end, or would you be doing the happy dance because you're no longer tied down to that person?

There's something called **Analysis Paralysis**. It's happened to most of us – you embark on a project, and start researching it, or working on it – but you never can finish the project. It may be a cluttered garage, painting a room, fixing an old car – or deciding to divorce your partner. I lived in my marriage for years, knowing that I wanted out, but too scared to make the move. Scared of being alone, scared of not having a nice place to live in, scared of my children being taken away from me. But eventually – I completed the project.

If you've decided to move on with the decision to divorce, or if that decision has been made for you, let's move on to the next section.

"Actually, I can."

~ Says YOU!

Pre-Divorce Checklist

First Steps

- ☐ When will you tell your partner? If they've already told you – this one is checked

- ☐ New private e-mail account – you don't have to use it right away, but it's a good idea

- ☐ Begin changing usernames and passwords for all accounts (social media, credit, banking, personal) – try not to use electronic means to keep track of everything, that can be hacked. Maybe a spiral notebook or a protected spreadsheet. Find a safe place to store the information on paper. If you have issues with privacy, you might want to store the information electronically, but be very sure that the storage is safe and private. There are a number of smart phone apps you can access, such as 1Password

- ☐ Find an attorney – ask around, call and talk to staff and get a feel for the office. Try www.lawyers.com and www.avvo.com

- ☐ Make appointment with the attorney that you choose (it's okay to visit with more than one)

- ☐ Decide who to tell – friends/family (It's always best to tell your partner first, but if you are in a potentially dangerous situation, you may need to tell your family before you tell your partner if safety is/may be an issue)

- ☐ Scout out places to live if you will move

- ☐ Begin your planning – what will be the timeline of your divorce, what will happen, and when

Financial Steps

- ☐ Budget your money with Mint (app available on iTunes or Google Play) or something similar. Mint also has a web-only interface.

- ☐ Stash some cash – you never know, you may need access to cash if your bank account(s) and credit cards get frozen, or closed without your knowledge

- ☐ Write down/gather all household bills

- ☐ Make a list of all joint financial accounts and current balances

Belongings

- ❑ List all household goods and belongings (everything, even stuff with no discernible value). Use the <u>Assets/Debts Spreadsheet</u> referenced on page 56. You can also download the document from www.dragongempublishing.com/launchyourdivorce.

- ❑ Safely store special personal items if needed – ask a friend, neighbor or family member to help

Children

- ❑ Think about, and decide now, who will get primary custody

- ❑ Read articles and books about telling children about divorce (resources listed later in the book)

- ❑ Decide how/when to tell your child about the divorce

CHAPTER THREE

Legal Matters

Choosing a Legal Professional

Choosing your attorney can be very important, or it may just be a minor step - it all depends on the scope of your case. Ask around, ask who other people used, ask what they liked, what they disliked.

You may be too embarrassed to ask anyone - that's okay. Get on the internet, most attorneys are listed, and have reviews of their work posted. Try www.lawyer.com or www.avvo.com. Read through the reviews. Look for comments that are related to what's important to you. Quick, fast, family-oriented, helped with custody problems, slam dunk, saved me, whatever it is that you're looking for, look for that type of comment.

List Your Legal Contact Possibilities

Name   Phone Number

_____   _____

_____   _____

_____   _____

Gather several names to interview, and make appointments. Sometimes the office staff will quote the cost of services, sometimes not. A non-contested case with a typical per hour billing of $250 for six to ten hours of work may be $2500 USD (that's United States dollars), and that may or may not include the court filing fees. They may give you different quotes for cases involving children. If there are other issues involved, you won't get a quote over the phone, they'll refer you to interview with an attorney or a paralegal.

What questions do you want to ask your legal professional?

_____

_____

_____

_____

_____

_____

_____

_____

_____

In order to have a non-contested case, you must satisfy the following criteria:

- ✓ All household belongings and property assets must be divided and agreed upon.
- ✓ All child custody matters must be agreed upon.
- ✓ If alimony is applicable, alimony amounts must be agreed upon.
- ✓ If civil or military retirement is applicable, those amounts must be agreed upon.
- ✓ If there are any investments to be divided, those must be agreed upon.
- ✓ If there are any debts to be divided, those must be agreed upon.

You may choose to enter into an Arbitrated Divorce Agreement, where an arbitrator assists you in making these agreements prior to signing the final documentation and presenting the agreements to the court. In any case – all of these must be fully agreed in order to have a non-contested divorce.

A contested divorce is when one or both partners cannot come to an agreement about the terms of the divorce, and a battle ensues. A contested divorce can double, triple, or drive the cost of the case into astronomical bounds. If this table or that plate is really worth it, then go for it. Otherwise, it's just stuff.

If the issue is child custody – yes, it may be worth it.

If the issue is alimony – it really depends on the situation and history of the marriage, and the verbal and non-verbal agreements made between the partners. If one partner agreed to put their education off until the other partner finished, and then children came along – and then twenty years later the uneducated partner wants a hefty alimony settlement because they didn't get a fancy education – can you blame them?

But if the alimony is because one partner doesn't want to work, and feels that they have "earned" a certain lifestyle simply by being married… In Texas we have a phrase for that. The phrase is "that dog don't hunt." In other words – you may recall reading this earlier – marriage is a 100/100% proposition (as opposed to 50/50%). The marriage didn't fail because of one partner's shortcomings, it failed because BOTH partners didn't live up to expectations. Pick yourself up, dust yourself off, and be a grownup. You can earn your own living. You may still be entitled to some alimony amount, but don't fight to relieve your partner of ALL of their disposable income. They have just as much right as you do to live in a decent living space.

 Do you live in an Alimony state? Find out by going to this great online resource: www.divorcesource.net – use the dropdown to choose your state.

DIY, or Do It Yourself Divorce

This is most likely **not** a do-it-yourself project. If you shared stuff, and have been together for a while, a legal professional is your best bet. On the Do-It-Yourself Divorce Forms and Forums that you find online – yes, these are often the forms that an attorney will use. However, in many regions, each county, parish, state or region often has their own rules and regulations about which forms apply to specific circumstances, so it's best to use an attorney to complete the forms and submit them appropriately.

Sharing the Same Attorney

Do not get talked into sharing the same attorney - DON'T! You may hear the phrase - "It'll save us money, it'll be cheaper, come on, we're friends..." When you are splitting up/going through a divorce, the mood may be friendly, but you are not friends. Protect your financial interests, and get your own attorney. You will hear of people that had successful, friendly divorces, and shared the same attorney – these are very few, and very far between. ONLY attempt this type of a divorce if you have NO children and NO property to argue over.

What if I can't afford $2500 for a divorce?

The good news is that most attorneys will work with you, and as long as you can give them a chunk of money each month, they're good with it. Most of them will not file the final paperwork until the whole bill is paid, but some will allow you to pay it out if you need to get out of the relationship and can demonstrate ability to pay. Most states have some type of waiting period before the final papers can be filed, see if your lawyer can take payments.

What if I can't afford to pay anything at all?

Many areas have Legal Aid Societies where local attorneys will do pro bono work (which means they will volunteer their skills for free). You may also live near a college or university with a law

school, and they may offer clinics where your case is mainly handled by a law student, but heavily supervised by a licensed attorney.

My cousin/family member is a lawyer, can he or she do my divorce?

If your cousin or other family member is certified as a family law practitioner, then that is an option. Family Law (in some cases, the divorce is handled by a Matrimonial Attorney) is a specialty, and you should be sure that your attorney is well versed in the most current statutes and regulations regarding the dissolution of marriages and civil unions, as well as child custody issues. A criminal lawyer should not be handling a divorce case (even though your soon-to-be-ex may be a thug, the regulations are vastly different between criminal law and family law!)

My partner is/was in the military or civil service, and has a pension. Can my lawyer draw up the papers for that?

Maybe. Some Family Law practitioners are better versed in QUADROS regulations than others, ask first. You may need to hire a separate attorney or financial advisor to draw up the paperwork for a pension division, especially for military and civil service. More information in the section on Military Divorce.

I am currently pregnant but want to divorce anyway, is that a problem?

Well, it does play into the child custody part of the case. Be sure your attorney is aware of the pregnancy, especially if there is any question of paternity - as in the father is not your current partner.

I am currently paying child support on a past divorce, and am getting divorced again, and will be paying even more child support. Will I be paying double?

That depends. It depends on what State you currently reside in, what state the original Child Support Order was executed in, what state the new Child Support Order will be executed in, and how much income you have. There are a lot of moving pieces in your situation, you need to consult with your attorney. Generally speaking, your wages cannot be garnished to the point that your take home pay is less than the prevailing minimum wage. If you are behind in payments, you need to let your attorney know.

I have a signed pre-nuptial agreement that has certain stipulations on it. What do I do?

That depends. It depends on what the stipulations are – generally, unless you signed under duress, were underage or other extenuating circumstance, the agreement stands. Be sure you advise your attorney of the agreement and bring a copy with you on the first visit.

What happens when I see the lawyer for the first time?

Typically, they'll ask you questions, get your driver's license information, where you work, your partner's personal information and work status. They'll get information about any children that you have. Be prepared with:

- ✓ Social Security Numbers – you, your partner, and your child/children

- ✓ Pay stubs for you, and maybe your partner (to establish salary)

- ✓ Tax return for the past year

- ✓ List of all assets (checking and savings accounts, household furnishings, cars, boats, houses, retirement accounts, real property)

- ✓ List of all debts (credit cards, loans, mortgages, etc.)

- ✓ Down payment or retainer – you should bring at least $250, $500 is better. $1000 is best. DO NOT LET MONEY stop you from seeing an attorney. Go in broke, but at least go to the appointment.

If you can bring all of this information to the very first meeting with your attorney, the legal team can start the filing process right away. What typically happens when the initial papers are filed (there may be more steps depending on your region and your situation):

- Attorney files a Petition for Divorce (there may be a different term for the action in your region). The person filing is the Plaintiff or Petitioner.
- The petition typically states that the Respondent (which is the person being sued for divorce) has a limited time to respond to the action. The Respondent should obtain legal counsel during that period to file a response.

- If no Response is filed, the laws may allow for a Summary Judgement to be obtained, which grants the Plaintiff/Petitioner the divorce.

- Separate issues include Alimony, Child Support and Child Insurance coverage. If the Respondent is being sued for any of these items, a Summary Judgement can be figured based on reasonable and allowable amounts. However, even though the court awards the Petitioner such amounts, there is no guarantee of collecting these amounts, that's an important concept.

- Pension – if either or both partners have a pension, there will be a QUADROS filing to divide the proceeds of that pension. You may need to hire a specialized attorney for that part of the divorce if your attorney doesn't have experience in that kind of process.

Contacting Your Attorney

THIS IS IMPORTANT – PLEASE READ THIS

You have to stay in contact with your attorney when it comes to anticipated deadlines. What does this mean? The following list shows reasons to contact your attorney. Keep in mind that you will probably billed every time you call your attorney – so don't go overboard.

GOOD Reasons to contact (call or e-mail) your attorney:

- You are expecting or expected them to file a document with the court and have not heard from your attorney by phone or by e-mail (they will usually send you a copy of the filed document)

- You are expecting a response from your partner's attorney with regards to a question and you have not heard from your attorney

- You are expecting to hear of a scheduled court date from your attorney and you have not heard from them

- Your partner has reneged (which means they aren't doing what they said they would do) on a previously written and filed document with the court with regards to temporary support (living expenses paid to you) during the course of the divorce, or temporary child custody

- Your contact information changes – such as phone number, mailing address, or living address

- Your job or income situation changes and you are unable to abide by previously agreed upon temporary support (living expenses paid to your partner) during the course of the divorce, or even pending alimony agreements, assets and debts distribution

-
  - <u>Your partner has threatened to physically harm you and/or your children</u> – call the police, and call your attorney immediately

You may notice that several of these reasons include the phrase "you have not heard from them". This is very common – your attorney has a lot of cases. Your case is typically not the first case on their list. If you think that they want your case to be over and finished with quickly – you are most likely mistaken. They will typically not push the path of your divorce along unless they hear from you on a regular basis – especially if you are on a payment plan. It is up to you to push the project.

These are NOT good reasons to contact your attorney

- Your partner has made a nasty comment and made you mad – Both of you need to grow up and act like adults.

- Your kids have threatened to go live with your partner instead of you because you won't give them something that they want – You need to parent your child/children, they are acting like spoiled brats.

Religious Divorce

This book in NO WAY discusses religious divorce procedures. In some religions, you may file for an annulment, even if there are children of the union. This is a long, drawn out process that may take years to go through the applicable religious courts. Some religions have rules about the female partner's rights in the divorce – such as financial considerations established at the beginning of the marriage to protect her and her children in the event of a dissolution. Be sure that you engage a religious attorney in situations like this.

"There comes a day when you realize turning the page is the best feeling in the world, because you realize there is so much more to the book than the page you were stuck on."

~ Zayn Malik

Chapter Four

Creating Your Divorce Plan

Merriam Webster Dictionary ~ A blueprint is a detailed plan of how to do something.

Divorces are typically date driven. This means that once you begin the process, there are certain dates that you will observe as you move the process along. Some of the dates are determined by you or your partner, other dates are determined by the attorneys and the courts.

> **Your Divorce Plan is simply YOUR personally written plan for how YOU plan and expect for YOUR divorce to happen.**
>
> **The path and timeline may not exactly follow your written plan – but just as a blueprint gives a construction crew guidelines and expectations for constructing a building, your plan gives YOU guidelines and expectations for de-constructing your relationship.**
>
> **Use the resources in this book to account and prepare for the unexpected.**

Whether you define yourself as an organized person, or a dis-organized person, your divorce is like any other project that you have ever done, or ever will do. I encourage you to try and **approach it as a project.** When you met your partner, he or she was most likely a project, a person that you consciously courted, made promises to, and most likely had a ceremony that included family and friends where you cemented your relationship.

A divorce is a similar concept, only you are **deconstructing** many parts, if not all parts, of the relationship. Let's talk about how your divorce project has milestones, which can be date driven if you want the process to finalize and be done with. One you tell your partner that you want a divorce, or your partner tells YOU that they want a divorce, there are some things that need to start happening.

- ✓ If you are initiating or expecting a divorce, don't be blind-sided. Plan things out. **Don't let someone else take control of your future, your destiny.** Be pro-active about the process, whether you are initiating the divorce, or your partner has initiated the process.

- ✓ This workbook includes a **Pre-Divorce Checklist.** Go through the list, print it out, and start checking off the key points that apply to your situation.

- ✓ Make an appointment with an attorney

- ✓ Take your **Pre-Divorce Checklist** items in the Financial section to your first appointment – this speeds up the discovery process

- ✓ Follow-up as soon as possible with the things your attorney asks you for

- ✓ Sign any court documents to be filed

- ✓ Attend any court hearings as scheduled

- ✓ Sign any final court documents to be filed

- ✓ Follow through any tasks that occur

I encourage you to adhere to the dates as much as you can to move the process along satisfactorily. Some of the tools that I use currently to organize my life include:

AwesomeNote

This is a goal setting tool for your smart phone that syncs with your calendar. It gives you the tools to set goal dates and appointment dates for things that you need to do, to attend, or to get done. You can create multiple folders to organize your goals – I have a Daily Checklist, a This Week Checklist, a Next Week Checklist, and a This Quarter Checklist. Some of these are simple To-Do items, some are date and time sensitive. I may create special folders for special events in my life – I anticipate marrying off one of my daughters soon, and when that process begins I will have a Wedding Checklist for her.

You may create a Divorce tab with date a to-do items – this can help you take care of all of the items needed to get this project moving, and keep it going in a timely fashion.

Outlook

I do have a Microsoft Outlook account that is used for one of my projects, and it can be used to give goal times for responses to e-mails, and have its own folders for correspondence to do with special projects. If you already use this tool, and can receive personal e-mail on that account, I suggest that you create a sub-folder in your Inbox to file your divorce correspondence for ready access and reference.

Google Calendar

This will also sync across devices, or you can use the web-access only

Privacy

If privacy is an issue (as in people are getting into your devices or accounts without your permission and without your knowledge), make sure that you create new accounts with new usernames, and new passwords. Password protect your devices to keep the information secure if your partner is snooping around in your business. It's not their business anymore.

Going Old School

I've mentioned a lot of computer and smart phone based tools – you can also use a spiral notebook, a moleskin notebook, a composition notebook, a diary. Anything that can keep track of dates, tasks, and other notes is just fine. Be sure to keep it close, and keep it safe and away from prying eyes.

I've also included some blank calendar pages in the back of this workbook, you can use those to keep track of divorce stuff – just be sure you look at it regularly if you keep a personal or work calendar as well! Best practice – incorporate the divorce tasks and meetings into your current calendaring practices.

What are some things that you need to do to move along in your divorce planning?

_____

_____

_____

_____

_____

_____

_____

CHAPTER FIVE

What to Say to Family, Friends and Employers

You may be a very public person – and everyone already knows your business. If so, you may want to dial it down a bit and soften your stance. Divorce isn't easy for anyone, don't poison any paths or burn any bridges unless absolutely necessary.

Regardless of how public or private a person you are, read through the following points as you are formulating your statements and responses to questions from your family, friends and employers:

1. Have your key talking points ready to go.
2. Avoid announcing the split on social media, unless absolutely necessary. Wait until the process is completed.
3. DO NOT SMACK TALK YOUR PARTNER. It's really for the best.
4. Make sure the timing is good for each person that you are speaking with.

Talking Points - Practice what you're going to say in different situations.

- My partner and I are splitting, and I appreciate your understanding as I work through this difficult time.
- I have filed for divorce OR My partner has filed for divorce – and I'm not ready to talk about it, but I wanted you to know.

Some people may immediately want to sit and talk with you about what happened, who was at fault, and they may want you to vent to them. Think first – is this person respectful of your privacy? Will they tell your private thoughts and history to someone that you'd rather not share such information with? Be cautious about airing your gripes, complaints, and emotions.

- Thank you for your concern, but I'd rather not discuss my relationship at this time.

If you have a best friend or family member that you feel you can confide in, then go for it – cry, scream, let them know how you feel. If you don't have that kind of support available, consider visiting with a professional counselor about your feelings.

Social Media – We'll discuss this more later in the workbook, but best practice is to not vent about your partner. You may consider changing your status to "It's Complicated" until your divorce is final.

Smack Talking Your Partner – Just don't. You're better than that.

<u>Timing</u> – You may not need to tell anyone right away. You may have to engage immediately – it all depends on your circumstances.

If you believe your partner may try to contact family/friends/employers about the divorce – then you should contact those people first. Let them know what is going on, and that they may be contacted. Ask them to support both you and your partner in this difficult time – and leave it at that.

If your partner has a vindictive streak, and you believe they may try to say negative things about you – be sure you let family, friends and employers know that your partner is having a difficult time, and they may receive some negative information as a result of the divorce. Ask them to let you know if they have any concerns or if any issues arise.

CHAPTER SIX

Where Will You Live?

Where will you live during the split-up, and after? Will you remain in the domestic home, or will you need to vacate? If you have your own money, this usually isn't a huge problem, more like an inconvenience. If you don't have your own money, this can make you believe that you can't afford to split from your partner. Don't get caught in that trap. There are always options. Unfortunately, the options available may cause "loss of face" and may sting your pride. Ditch the pride. Take your knocks, and get out. Move in with a friend or a family member. Make arrangements to go into a protective shelter. In some situations, it can save your life, and/or the lives of your children.

Apartment Search Engines:

www.apartments.com

www.apartmentsearch.com

You can also look at your local newspaper. Many convenience stores will have a Thrifty Nickel paper version, or in larger metro areas, you'll find bound apartment and rent house magazines.

Things you want to keep in mind as you are apartment or house-hunting:
- ❖ What is your price range? _____
- ❖ How many bedrooms do you need? _____
- ❖ Do you need a fenced yard? _____
- ❖ Will you have pets? _____
- ❖ Do you need access to a swimming pool? _____
- ❖ Do you need access to a playground? _____
- ❖ Do you need close proximity to community amenities (schools, groceries) _____

Do I Have To Move Out As Soon As We Announce That We Are Divorcing?

Not always. In some cases, if you have an amicable split, you can remain under the same roof as your partner until one or both of you have secured alternate arrangements. Usually, moving out of the shared bed and bedroom is customary, if possible. If there are children of the union, it may be a good idea to stay in the communal home as long as possible in order to keep an ongoing relationship with the children. Sleeping on the couch, in the study, or in a child's room is an option.

Moving out can be complicated by a shared mortgage, a home not selling in a reasonable time-frame, lack of available housing, or lack of appropriate housing. Don't give up, keep trying. A short-sale on a home may be better than a foreclosure. Taking a short-term lease until something better comes along is also an option. Cousin Betty's sofa might look pretty good after a while... You may also choose to lease the home to a renter while both of you move into alternate spaces. This can allow the home to increase in value, or for the mortgage to be paid down so as not to lose so much money if you are upside-down on the loan.

Can My Partner Kick Me Out?

Your partner may have been to seek professional legal assistance first, and they may have filed a court order that prohibits you from being within a certain geographical distance of them, or of their residence. This, in effect, kicks you out of your home. So, yes, they can. You can seek professional legal assistance, as well, and have the court order rescinded, overturned, or dismissed (all kinds of legal terminology in that field - get an attorney). You can play the game that your partner started - but it's best to not play. Just get your possessions, and leave, if at all possible. Take pictures of anything that you cannot take with you for whatever reason, and include them with your list of Assets that you would like to retain in the settlement - make sure that your attorney is aware of your wishes from the beginning. We'll discuss Assets, Debts, and Dividing Possessions in another chapter.

Where Will My Child Live?

Many states, regions, counties and parishes allow joint custody, so in essence, your children can have a room in your house, and in your soon-to-be-ex-partner's house. However, every situation and circumstance is different, and the court has the ultimate say regarding where your child will reside if you and your partner cannot come to an agreement on child custody arrangements. There are some great books on Amazon, please check the Resources in the children's section. You can buy books on Kindle to read, but you can also order them online. Your local book store or library may have a section on helping kids deal with divorce. Be sure that the books you get for your kids are age appropriate in nature – in other words, **YOU** read them first, and make sure that the message that you want your kids to have is in the book or books.

"We ruined each other by being together. We destroyed each other's dreams."

~ Kate Chisman, Run

CHAPTER SEVEN

Helping Children Cope

Kids add an entirely new dimension to the proceedings. They add pages and pages to the final judgment, and the resulting monetary judgments to do with child support, and health care responsibility may cause partners to continue harsh words after the split up is considered complete by the court system.

Some of you will stay together "for the children". I know – I did that, too. And it may work for you, for a while. But do you really want your children to grow up thinking that your dysfunctional marriage is how THEIR marriage should work when they grow up? Yeah, I thought not.

Your Child's Self Esteem

Many children will try to blame themselves for their parents' breakup. Do everything you can to convince them otherwise, in a loving and understanding way. Also - and this may be difficult - do not "smack talk" your partner to the child. Half of your child's identity is from that other person, and your child may feel that any negative comments that you make about your partner (or ex-partner) reflect upon them - your child. If you have a young child, you may think you have to make up excuses on behalf of your partner to explain some behaviors. It's really best that your child understand pretty quickly how it's going to work. You can tell your child, I'm sorry that you are disappointed, but daddy/mommy did not/will not be doing _____ (insert whatever your ex isn't doing). It doesn't mean that he/she doesn't love you. Express this with full eye contact, while touching their arm or shoulder if your child likes to be touched, and you might sit or crouch to be on their level.

Professional Counseling

If you are leaving an abusive relationship (whether physical, verbal or mental), you MUST get your child some professional counseling. Your child will have memories of the split up for the rest of his/her life - do what you can to make it as smooth as possible.

Even the best of divorces can leave hidden scars. If your child begins to act out at school or while playing with others, or exhibits behaviors that you aren't used to them showing, counseling may help them work through their issues with regards to your break-up. Counseling may be available through your religious affiliation if you can't afford traditional counseling, ask around for assistance.

Children's Books on Divorce

Two Homes - By Claire Masurel
Ages: 3 – 7 Years

Standing on My Own Two Feet - By Tamara Schmitz
Ages: 4 and up

It's Not Your Fault, Koko Bear - By Vicky Lansky
Ages: 3 – 7 Years

Dinosaurs Divorce - By Marc Brown
Ages: 3 – 6 Years

Divorce is Not The End of the World - By Zoe Stern
Ages: 8 – 12

Mom's House, Dad's House for Kids - By Isolina Ricci, Ph.D.
Ages: This is for kids that are capable of reading a longer book, so it could be for an adventurous 7 year old, but it can explain things to some hurting 18 year olds, too.

What In the World Do You Do When Your Parents Divorce? - By Kent Winchester, J.D.
Ages: 8 - 12

Books on Co-Parenting-and other Divorce Topics

Divorce: How to Tell Your Kids
By Damon Martin

Vicky Lansky's Divorce Book for Parents: Helping Your Child Cope
By Vicky Lansky

Mom's House, Dad's House: Making Two Homes for Your Child
By Isolina Ricci, Ph.D.
Note that this is the companion book to the children's book mentioned previously.

**Please note that there are many more books available in your public library and local bookstores.

Child Custody

Oh, what a tangled web we weave. Every circumstance is different, but many states, regions, counties and parishes are the same. Joint custody is often an option, but usually one parent is designated as the primary parent, and that is usually where the child spends the majority of his/her nights. Some states will allow a weekday and a weekend day alternate custody schedule, or every other weekend, alternating year holidays, secondary parent may have the child/children for six weeks over the summer break, etc. This is often a heavily negotiated settlement, make sure that the person or people that come out best in the arrangement is/are your child/children. Don't negotiate this on your own, have an attorney handle this part of the divorce.

Child Support

Child Support can be based on the non-custodial or secondary parent's income or salary level, or it can be based on the number of days that they have the child in their possession during the year, or a combination of the two. Each state has different calculations, check with your attorney. There are also a boat-load of state-specific smart phone apps available to download to help calculate child support, you may want to look into apps that apply to your specific region for more information.

Question: I'm Behind Paying Child Support - Can My Ex Keep Me From Seeing My Child?

Answer: That depends on the region that you are in, but usually not. Child Support is not payment in order to see the child, it is payment to assist with the living expenses for your child, including housing, food, clothing, school supplies and expenses, entertainment, etc. If you are being denied the right to see your child for any reason, you can contact your attorney, or the Court, and have your ex-partner cited for Contempt of Court (in some cases). Depending on how far behind you are in your Child Support payments and the reason for the arrears, you may be opening up a different can of worms by doing this. In almost all regions, you can be jailed, lose your Driver's License and any State-issued Professional Certifications for falling behind in Child Support payments. You may need to lay low and avoid the court as you seek employment to meet your obligation.

Child Health Care

Many low income children qualify for State funded low cost/no cost health care or Medicaid. Make sure your child is enrolled if they qualify. If you have a Divorce Decree or other official document that states that your ex-partner is responsible for carrying your child's health insurance, make sure that your child is enrolled on that policy. Contact the insurer, and get yourself listed as a contact on the policy so that you are made aware if the policy is cancelled or it lapses for any reason. Always get an insurance card so that YOU can take your child to the doctor, or to the hospital. Your ex-partner may insist that THEY will take care of that, but it is crucial that you BOTH have access to medical care for your child at all times.

CHAPTER EIGHT

During the Divorce Checklist

Continuing General Steps

- ❑ Implement new private e-mail account for personal use

- ❑ Change all passwords (usernames if possible) on financial accounts

- ❑ Tell your family/friends. You may just want to tell a select few, some don't need to know until it's all done and finished. Some will want to hold your hand right away – tell those people.

- ❑ Inform your employer of your pending status if necessary. If your partner may cause problems, your employer (as in your immediate supervisor) needs to be aware of what may happen.

- ❑ _____

- ❑ _____

- ❑ _____

- ❑ _____

If You Have To Move

- ❑ Sign lease at new living space.

- ❑ Notify current landlord of move-out date.

- ❑ Box up belongings.

- ❑ Contact moving company or friends and family to help with the move.

- ❑ Help partner move out (or not).

- ❏ Change mailing address with the postal service.
- ❏ _____
- ❏ _____

Financial Steps

- ❏ Notify credit cards of the divorce (and new address, if applicable).
- ❏ Close joint accounts.
- ❏ Notify mortgage holder of divorce and new mailing address
- ❏ Re-Finance mortgage if needed
- ❏ Establish separate checking and savings accounts
- ❏ _____
- ❏ _____
- ❏ _____
- ❏ _____

Belongings/Possessions

- ❏ Separate yours and theirs.
- ❏ Wait until final decree for some items to be separated.
- ❏ Negotiate for some possessions that weren't specified in the court decree.
- ❏ If all else fails, it's just stuff, pretend it burned, and move on.
- ❏ _____
- ❏ _____
- ❏ _____
- ❏ _____

Children

- ❑ Do not smack talk your partner in front of your child (or anyone else, keep it private if possible).
- ❑ Offer/obtain counseling for your child.
- ❑ Notify school or daycare if necessary.
- ❑ Buy them/read them books to help them deal with the divorce.
- ❑ _____
- ❑ _____
- ❑ _____
- ❑ _____

Budgeting

First thing

Download a budgeting program. I recommend <u>Mint by Intuit</u>. (It's free to use, you'll get some junk e-mail inviting you to try other financial products. You can use it online, with an iPhone or Android app, or all of the above – <u>www.mint.com</u>.) Mint hooks into all of your bank accounts, retirement accounts and credit cards, and sends you alerts reminding you to pay stuff, and shows you where you're spending your money. Easiest budget tool ever. It will hook up to your retirement account and take you through projected retirement scenarios, tell you if you're saving enough. (I've saved enough to sit on the steps and feed birds when I retire - unfortunately, I have to sleep on that step, too…)

Nobody likes to "live on a budget". Yet it's something that we all do, every single one of us. Initiating a budget can be painful and scary, but it can also be enlightening and freeing. Start by taking a look at your current lifestyle. If you need to cut corners, examine everything. Look over the following to start with:

Housing

Do you really need a four-bedroom house/apartment? Can you give up that guest room or office and downsize to a smaller and cheaper living space? Since you'll be sleeping alone, can your bedroom double as an office space? Can a corner of the kitchen, or breakfast room, or living room be set aside as your office space? In some very temporary situations, you may share a room or a bed with your child to save money and space. Depending on your culture and your socio-economic level, this may be a normal situation. It ***could become*** a normal situation if you're really trying to live on a budget.

List ways you can or might save money on housing:

_____

_____

_____

_____

_____

Transportation

If you have a good chunk of equity in your car but are still making payments - is it worth it to pay it off and keep it? Or could you trade it in on something smaller or older for the equity amount to stop making payments? Do you really need a car? If you live in a city with good public transportation, you may be able to sell the car entirely and stash the money in savings or pay off some outstanding debt.

If you already own a car, think of ways you can save money by maintaining it correctly. Do you really need to use premium fuel? Are you on a maintenance schedule for oil changes, air filter changes, tire pressure checks and tire rotation? Are you protecting the finish with regular washing and waxing? Do you clean and deodorize the inside of the car to keep the value of the vehicle?

List ways you can or might save money on transportation:

_____

_____

_____

Television entertainment

Do you really need over 300 choices of cable or satellite video and music choices with 35 movie channels? Think of down-sizing your package, or getting rid of it entirely and using local channels. Netflix and HuluPlus are internet options for seeing some of your "can't miss" shows a little later in the season. Might be worth it to save a hundred bucks a month. This may interfere with your internet provider package, so you may have to just get creative and choose a cheaper package to retain your internet. Or borrow a neighbor's signal (ask first!)

List ways you can or might save money on television entertainment:

_____

_____

_____

Satellite radio

Depending on where you live - there really are local radio stations that play music... And many cars built recently have accessory ports that you can plug an mp3 player into to listen to your own music. Pandora has a free version on the internet – one of my faves.

Land-line Telephone/Cellular Phone Service

More and more people are giving up their land-line phones and just have a cell phone. For some of us this won't work, because our internet is tied to our home phone package. Cellular phone companies vary widely in their monthly charges, and also on the upgrade timeframe – shop around for the best deal, and think carefully about using a cheaper provider if their service or coverage isn't what you really need.

List ways you can or might save money on telephone/cellular phone service:

_____

_____

_____

_____

Groceries

Yeah, I hate getting stuck behind the coupon lady, too. But it is important to price compare when you are shopping. One thing to keep in mind - if the majority of your food does not come in a box, your food bill is going to be cheaper, and you will be healthier. Try to eat a lot of fresh vegetables, some bargain fruits, and watch for bargains on unprocessed meats (if you're inclined to eat meat). Watch ads for sales on dairy products and other specialty items that you really like. Your city may also have a "dented can or box" store that sells damaged packaged products at a discount. Look for "day old" bakery stores or outlets. Look for Farmer's Markets on Saturday mornings, or sometimes on advertised weekdays – these can be a great source of locally grown produce. Watch prices on ALL "bargain" foods, they're not always cheaper than the grocery store! And keep in mind - buying in bulk is not always a bargain. I love Costco as much as anyone, but do I really need 20 pounds of jasmine rice?

One thing you should do - watch Craigslist or your local Classifieds for a used freezer. Depending on your available space, you can get one the size of a small dishwasher, or if you have more space – get one that's larger. When items go on sale that can be frozen - stock up. I once found packaged hot dogs for 25 cents a pack - gross, but I was poor and the kids thought I was the best mom EVER that summer. And that fall. And winter...

Casseroles are very hearty and usually cheap to make (depending on the ingredients), and leftovers can be refrigerated or frozen in individual packages for many non-egg based items. Rice-based items do well, sometimes pasta items are mushy when thawed and re-heated. Corn tortilla based casseroles do pretty well - flour ones get gummy.

List ways you can or might save money on groceries:

_____

_____

_____

_____

Bag It, Baby

Watch your "eating out" expenses. When you make dinner, make enough to take for lunch the next day or two (be sure to pack and carry in Pyrex (glass) or mason (canning) jars, not plastic Tupperware type containers – many carcinogens – which cause cancer – are released when heating food in plastic!). Buy sandwich ingredients at the store. Keep canned soup and a can-opener in your desk at work. Eat ramen noodles. Eat bread and peanut butter. If you travel for a living - stay at hotels with a free breakfast, and grab English Muffins, peanut butter and jelly or bananas - FREE LUNCH! (Also, you can grab boiled eggs and stash them in a to-go coffee cup, they'll be good for a few hours). Other hotel breakfast items you can stash for later include sausage and bacon, muffins, salsa, mustard and mayonnaise, fresh fruit, yogurt, milk containers, biscuits.

List ways you can or might save money on meals outside of the home:

_____

_____

_____

_____

Diapers

If you have the time, invest in some cloth diapers. It may take a few months to collect enough - and get some diaper wraps to hold them on your baby/toddler. This can save money, especially if you have more than one in diapers at a time. Shake out the solids in the toilet. One rinse cycle to shake loose the leftovers (try using a vinegar soak to get some of the urine out here). Full wash cycle with bleach and detergent. Final rinse with fabric softener. Dry on clothesline (saves money!) or in the dryer. Yes, it can be done, even if you're working full time. Buck up, Bambi.

Baby Food

That jar stuff is plain nasty! Take real, unseasoned food, put it through the food processor (or use a blender like I did, I was too poor for a food processor). Spoon the mess into ice cube trays, and freeze. Pop the food-sicles into a gallon sized zipped plastic storage bag. Label the bag. Thaw as needed! Oatmeal, brown rice, meats, cooked veggies and fruits (canned fruits make this a breeze, choose fruits packed in unsweetened juice) are great choices here. I was very lucky, my family was heavy into canning, and made me jars of apple sauce and pear sauce when my babies were small.

List ways you can or might save money on baby food:

_____

_____

_____

_____

Government Food Programs

Depending on your income level, you may qualify for government assistance to help with your housing, groceries, child care needs, and job re-training. Don't be afraid to ask! Also, there may be private and non-profit organizations that can help out if you don't qualify for government assistance (think religious organizations for the most part – you may have to put up with some evangelizing, but if it feeds and clothes your child, just nod yes and say "Amen"). Yes – it may be embarrassing. But it's better than being hungry, or cold, or without shelter for you and your child. Speak up! Look up some food programs in your area – if not for yourself, then programs you might donate to:

_____

_____

Buy It Used

That's right - your car, your appliances, your computer (really? yes, really), your clothes. Consignments stores, Salvation Army, Goodwill, Craigslist and eBay are my drug of choice on the used front. Know what you want, know what that item is really worth before you lay out the money for it. A "great deal" may not always be great if Best Buy, Lowes or Tiger Direct is offering an instant rebate on it brand new.

List ways you can or might save money by trying discount stores, buying used goods:

_____

_____

_____

Is It Always Wise To Go Cheap?

No. Some "bargain brand" items are not the equivalent to the stuff next to it on the shelf. You'll figure it out. It's like Old Navy jeans next to Levi's. Yeah, the Old Navy jeans may be cheaper - but they'll most likely wear out faster. Is that really a bargain? Not in my book. Goodwill might have a pair of those Levi's - I'm not proud. Nor should you be.

Some people are embarrassed about money, or rather, their lack of money. You can always "make" or earn more money. Money is temporary.

Write down your fears about money and divorce – let it all out. Vent. Make sure that you understand for yourself what your fears are – about being hungry, homeless. Are your fears that you won't be able to buy the best "stuff?" Or that you won't be able to enjoy the same standard of entertainment or living arrangements? Write it down, understand it, own the fear. Then get over it.

_____

_____

_____

_____

_____

Really? That's all? Write some more about your fears about money. Keep going. Don't cheat!

CHAPTER TEN

Dividing Assets & Debts

This discussion has sub-sections for Assets, Debts, and then using the Spreadsheet. To get yours, please visit www.dragongempublishing.com/launchyourdivorce.

Assets

The following sub-section contains short topical discussions with quick advice tidbits. None of this is a replacement for the advice of a qualified legal professional - which is highly recommended.

Separation of property should not be a Do-It-Yourself Project. Two terms you should be aware of - <u>equal</u>, and <u>equitable</u>. <u>Equal</u> means 50/50. <u>Equitable</u>, unfortunately, does not. If your state or geographic area is subject to the term <u>equitable</u> in divorce law, it means that the judge can take into account many factors when deciding how to divide property and debts. For instance, if one partner has a high paying job and the other does not work, the judge may award the majority of the assets to the non-working partner, because the working partner can re-accumulate assets, while the non-working partner may not be able to.

Keep those terms in mind when speaking with your legal professional and reviewing your regional laws regarding separation of marital property. You can also go to www.divorcesource.net for more information. Go there now, review the rules!

What state/territory are you divorcing in? _____

Do you live in a community property state/territory? _____

What About a Business Interest?

If you, or your partner, have an interest in a business (which means you own a business, or part of a business, or have invested in a business), get a current Profit and Loss Statement for the business. Get the last auditor's statement. Find out what the business is worth – and find out what the business interest is worth in Fair Market Value dollars. That has to be part of the Assets and Debt – if the business interest is in the NEGATIVE, that should be stated, as well (treat it like a debt).

Do you or your partner have a business, or a business interest? ❑ Yes ❑ No   ❑ I'm not sure…

If you or your partner have a business or an interest in a business, you'll need to get documents proving ownership and value to give to your legal professional.

How do I value or divide a pension or a 401(k) or IRA?

You don't. You probably get a quarterly statement, and may even have daily access to your balance. But you need an attorney that is competent in QUADROS actions to file that paperwork for you. QUADROS is an acronym that means Qualified Domestic Relations Order, and it's a legal term defining some of the documents that have to do with marriage dissolution. Don't do that on your own, it's tricky, and missing a deadline, especially with a government agency, can make a huge difference in getting what is due to you. The same with a military pension - you need an attorney that is very familiar with QUADROS actions so that you are not cheated out of your rightful pension, or your rightful share of your partner's pension. Things to watch out for - some attorneys will draft the QUADROS document to give the departing partner half of the pension amount, when they may actually be due a reduced percentage depending on the number of years of the marriage, or their share may be based on value of the pension at the date of the divorce. Know the law before you sign off on anything.

	Pension Value	401(k) Value	IRA Value
You	_____	_____	_____
Your Partner	_____	_____	_____

* Keep in mind that these values change from day to day. When it comes time to finalize the divorce, you might want to check on these figures before signing anything.

What if I'm in a same sex marriage or union?

As of the publication of this guide, many countries recognize same-sex unions, and they are treated no differently than a traditional union. If you were married in a country that recognizes same-sex unions, but have moved to a country that does not, you need an attorney to sort out the end of the relationship.

What about pets?

Pets, unfortunately, are considered property. Some courts will be lenient and allow visitation of pets, but most treat them as property, and will award them to one partner or the other. There are many stories with sad outcomes here - don't be one of them. Do what's best for your pet, and don't put them through a lot of drama.

How do I divide community property?

Some regions are designated as "community property" states, which means that property accumulated in a marriage must be divided equally, or at least equitably. Equally means 50/50 division of assets and debts. Equitably means that property should be divided based on need, based on who purchased it, or based on who put more into the marriage financially or with their personal efforts. The term "equitably" is what causes the most fights between separating partners, because the courts will take into consideration if one partner never worked but raised a family, or if a partner was proven to be cheating on the other partner. Attorneys can twist and morph the opposing partner into a monster, and cause great suffering to the entire family with vindictiveness.

You and your partner have three choices on community property.

1) You take it.

2) They take it.

3) You sell it and one or the other gets the proceeds, or you split them in some equal (or equitable) way depending on the way the rest of the settlement is going.

If you choose none of the above, the judge (Court) will choose for you. And it may not go the way either of you wants. The terms "equal" and "equitable" are not the same, keep that in mind. No two regions have exactly the same law - you really should seek legal counsel. Using Do-It-Yourself Divorce Kit forms from an office store or off of the internet is not the best option, unless you have no assets or debts or children whatsoever.

What about separate property acquired before or during the marriage?

In many states, including some of the so-called "community property" states, property held by individuals prior to the marriage, or received as a gift or inheritance during the marriage, is separate from communal or community property, and does not need to be listed in the Assets. Consult with your legal professional to find out if any of the Assets fall in this exception.

Debts

This is a short topical discussion about Debts, and is not in any way a replacement for advice from a legal professional. Dividing Assets and Debts should not be a Do-It-Yourself project.

Secured Debts

Debts are amounts owed to others - such as for money loaned to you to purchase a house, or a car. These types of debts are considered to be "secured" loans - they are "secured" by property, so that if the debtor falls behind or stops paying on the loan, the holder of the loan can seize, or repossess the property to recover the balance of the debt.

Unsecured Debts

Other loans may be "unsecured" - such as credit card debt, or "signature loans" or service loans for services rendered by a contractor for home repairs. These loans are granted based on your credit history or job history. There may be medical/hospital debt due to a health issue that wasn't covered by insurance.

Who Is Responsible?

Some debts belong to the partnership as a whole, such as a mortgage or car loan that has both partners' names on them. Some debts may have just one name on it. When splitting up, some courts may not care whose name is on the debt, if the debt was incurred during the partnership, then the debt belongs to the partnership. Other states may go by whose name is on the debt - it is best to consult a legal professional when splitting up the debt of the partnership. Depending on the Assets, one partner may be able to assume more debt if they are also assuming more Assets. Keep in mind that "equal" does not always mean the same thing as "equitable" when it comes to the law.

WARNING If you have a College Loan (or ANY DEBT) for a child - known as a PLUS Loan in one partner's name – the court may judge that both partners are equally liable for the debt. If YOU are the holder of the debt, DO NOT accept payments from your partner for the liability, GET THE MONEY UP FRONT. Have them get the money from their 401(k), or some other asset.

Courts may "judge" that you have to receive monthly payments until the debt is satisfied – but if the payments stop, it is costly to go after your ex-partner. Be smart get the money up front.

On the other side – if YOU are ordered to make monthly payments on a debt, keep in mind that **YOU MAY HAVE NO RECOURSE IF YOUR EX-PARTNER DOES NOT PAY THAT MONEY TO THE LOAN COMPANY!!!** You MUST ask for a monthly statement that shows your payment has been given to the loan company, and you MUST know UP FRONT how much YOUR SHARE of the payments are. Otherwise, you may be paying forever because your ex-partner isn't bothering to pay the debt AT ALL!!!

Who Is Responsible? (continued)

You can ask that your part of the debt be adjudicated separately so that you can make your payments directly to the creditor. Creditors may not be willing to re-do the terms of the loan, but a court order can direct them to take payments from separate payors. In the case of student loans, the website requires that each time you pay on the loan you input the loan holder's Social Security Number and date of birth - have the court order the creditor to establish a separate account with YOUR information so that you do not have to keep inputting your ex's information each month!

Tax Issues

You may find out late in the relationship or after your divorce that your partner had filed fraudulent tax returns, or not filed tax returns at all. Unfortunately, in many cases, you may end up being held responsible for any incurred tax liabilities during the marriage. Depending on the customs of your taxing region, you may be able to plead for a reduction of the liability or transfer of liability by using the "Innocent Spouse Defense". If you are facing a situation like this, you should retain a Tax Attorney to help defend you, if you are unable to just pay the liability and move on.

Do you have copies of the last seven years of tax filings for you and your partners? This isn't a yes or no question – just a heads up. You probably should have those records, and hold on to them after the divorce is finalized.

When it comes time to divide the property of the relationship, the courts are concerned with the following:

1) Property (Assets) and Debts

2) Income and Expenses

3) Children (This will also include Health Care Responsibility documents)

4) Name Change Request of Either Partner

This section has to do with identifying the information to input on the **Assets & Debts Spreadsheet** that is included with this program. Please visit www.dragongempublishing.com/launchyourdivorce to get yours – you do not have to sign up for a mailing list, there are no obligations to receiving the spreadsheet. The Spreadsheet is in Excel format - using Microsoft Excel is highly recommended. You can also use the spreadsheet application from www.openoffice.org – that is a free program. These are the guidelines for the spreadsheet use:

1) In the columns that report the dollar amounts that are being split up, you should change the YourName and PartnerName to **YOUR NAME** and **YOUR PARTNER'S** name

2) In the Assets/Debts column, you may type a name for each Asset/Debt/Business Interest.

3) In the Input Value column, input the NET VALUE of the Asset, or the AMOUNT OWED on the debt **_(remember to use a minus sign before or after the debt or negative Business Interest amount)_** or the FAIR MARKET VALUE of the Business Interest. If you haven't read the section on Assets, please do so. Input EVERYTHING, including family pictures, Christmas decorations, and family pets by name. Don't leave ANYTHING out. You do not have to place a value on everything, you may have zero value items, but it's easier to place a one dollar value on it so that the spreadsheet illustrates clearly WHO gets what.

4) The YOUR PERCENTAGE column adjusts the percentage amounts for BOTH partners, and automatically recalculates dollar amounts for BOTH partners.

5) If you HIGHLIGHT + RIGHT CLICK > INSERT a Row, be sure and do it where indicated near the bottom of the spreadsheet. AND you will need to COPY and PASTE the indicated Row to keep the formulas intact.

6) Don't be a jerk and input Assets or Debts with incorrect amounts. You'll get caught. Don't mess with the formulas. They're there to help everyone.

7) When you're ready to share your information, e-mail the entire spreadsheet to your legal professional. Or your partner. This is a worksheet. This can help you, and your partner, understand the scope and depth of your communal property. It can also help your legal professionals and the courts, if necessary, arrive at an equal and/or equitable division of that property.

Don't want to use a computer? You can draw up your own, or type it up. It should look something like this:

Asset | Debt | Business Name	Net Value	Your %	Your Value	Partner's %	Partner's Value
Ex: House on Elm Street	50,000	100%	50,000	0	0
Ex: 2005 Honda Accord	6,000	0	0	100	6,000
Ex: Your 401(k)	138,725	50%	69,362.5	50%	69.362.5
Ex: Capital One Visa	(2,748.26)	50%	(1,374.13)	50%	(1,374.13)
TOTALS					

CHAPTER ELEVEN

Military Divorce

There are a lot of considerations when it comes to divorce when one or both partners are in the military. The first thing - get your own lawyer. Be sure that your lawyer is well versed in military divorce - don't just take their word for it, start quizzing them on the following topics, and go somewhere else if you don't get good answers. Many military bases have family attorneys – you can use this type of representation to begin your divorce, or change to this method if you aren't satisfied with your current attorney. One thing that is commonly done by military spouses facing divorce is to go ahead and visit the base family attorney, even if you do not plan on using them for representation. Spouses will do this to "muddy the water" in case the other partner decides to use the base attorney, they will not be able to because the base attorney had prior knowledge of the pending divorce. Just be aware of this practice when beginning a contentious process.

Where to File?

There are two considerations when deciding where to file, residence and domicile. Most courts require filing in the jurisdiction where the military member is currently residing or has established residency. There can be conflicts when the military member has accepted a posting away from their family, so residency may be where the family resides - this is considered "domicile". A legal professional can help decide the issue. Some military members will "separate" from the spouse, and accept an assignment elsewhere in order to find more amenable laws for the divorce process and aftermath. For example, in some regions, alimony, or post-divorce spousal support, is a permanent fixation, while in many other regions, it is a temporary or limited payment system. A spouse could establish residency in a region that is more financially favorable to avoid long-term financial diminishment. Always consult an attorney to decide if this is the best path for the family.

Do the military member and the partner live in separate jurisdictions?   ❏ Yes ❏ No

If so, is the partner considered in the family domicile?   ❏ Yes ❏ No

Is there a reason to file in a different jurisdiction?   ❏ Yes ❏ No

Housing

Is the couple currently in base housing or sponsored housing? If a non-military partner will be awarded custody of children, the family will no longer qualify for base or sponsored housing, and will have to consider the cost of off-base housing. While on-base family housing is "issued" to the military member, the member does not have the authority to evict his/her military family members (only the installation commander has that authority). In fact, in most cases, when a domestic situation has deteriorated to the point where physical separation is warranted, the leading non-commissioned officer and/or base commander will usually order the military member to reside in the dormitory (barracks). This is because the military has the authority to house (for free) the military member in the dormitories, but it has no authority to provide free billeting to military spouses. However, military family housing, by law, can only be occupied by military members who reside with their family members (other than authorized exceptions, such as when the military member is deployed, at sea, or serving in a remote-tour area). The services all have regulations which require the family housing unit to be vacated (usually within 30 days) if the military members stops residing there, or if there are no family members residing there. So, in most cases, in the event of a separation, the party remaining in the base housing unit must vacate (unless the remaining party is the military member and other dependents, such as children, remain). The military will usually not pay for such moves, however, unless the divorce is not yet final, and the military member is transferring to a different post.

There may be some leeway in that situation, because typically the moves are by weight. You may be able to make part of the move, or move part of the weight to a different place, depending on the decisions made by the military member's "handler." Approach the handler with caution, and you may be able to accomplish both moves on the same set of orders.

Spousal Support

Typically in the military, one spouse will forego going to school or pursuing a career to care for the family. This becomes an issue in a divorce when the partner has no education or skills to support themselves. In many states, there are laws providing for temporary court ordered spousal support during and after a divorce to allow for retraining and education. Most states that do order spousal support (alimony) have a limit to the payments, there are few states that offer "permanent alimony". Some partners will make voluntary agreements in the divorce between themselves to provide for assistance with housing, car payments, tuition payments, and other living expenses. But these voluntary agreements are not the rule, and are strictly voluntary.

Child Support

Child support is granted on a region by region basis, and is granted according to the rules of the region where the divorce is granted. Child support is typically automatically withheld and paid, and usually military members don't get the chance to get behind on child support. In some jurisdictions, child support may be ordered past the child's eighteenth birthday as long as the child attends college full time during the school year. Check with your attorney if this needs to be a consideration.

Child Custody

With deployments being the rule rather than the exception in today's military, it is common and usual for the non-military member partner to have primary custody of the child(ren) of the relationship. In many states, shared custody is possible, but in the case of deployment, the partners need to agree in advance to the primary custody of the child reverting to the non-military partner, but to resume as shared upon the cease of the deployment. Language is very important in legal documentation, be sure that these issues are addressed appropriately.

Child Visitation

The same as the civilian community, child visitation is typically not tied to the payment of child support. Parents are encouraged to take advantage of the court ordered visitation dates, but partners can always negotiate for more or less visitation outside of the court order, depending on the circumstances. However, if the custodial parent does not abide by the established orders, the non-custodial parent usually does not have any legal recourse to enforce the order. Which means that you can't call the police and make your ex give you the kids for your weekend or your evening. It just doesn't work that way. You can spend a lot of money and start filing injunctions and civil suits for deprivation of parental rights, but you'll really be spinning your wheels. It's a very sad time when an ex-partner puts children in the firing line of a battle that they don't belong in.

Thrift Savings Plan (TSP)

A TSP (United States of America) is treated like a 401(k) retirement plan, and is subject to negotiation in the divorce proceedings. For instance, if the partners shared property, such as a home or other property, one partner might get the 401(k) and the other get the house.

Dividing the Pension

There are a lot of myths and misinformation about dividing up military pensions, and it's imperative that you have a lawyer that is well-versed in QUADROS law. QUADROS is an acronym for Qualified Domestic Relations Order. The ex-spouse cannot receive retiree pay until the retiree pay applies for it, and some divorces may stipulate timeframes that the retiree must apply for the pension. There have been documented cases when a military member has avoided applying for a pension so that their ex-spouse would not receive benefits - a bit extreme, but some breakups can be pretty bad and cause a lot of hard feelings. There are rules about how long the partners are married before they can claim a portion of the pension - again, be sure that your lawyer fully understands QUADROS law. If you are on the receiving end of the divorce, don't sign off on the QUADROS papers unless you've had a fabulous lawyer fully review the entire document. Just one sentence can make the difference in thousands of dollars in benefits - annually, and possibly monthly, depending on the size of the pension.

There are different methods of calculating what percentage of the pension to which ex-spouses are entitled. The document filed with the court will need to clearly state the formula used to derive the amount of payment. Again, the length of the marriage will come into play. One of the more common trends is to count the amount of points accumulated in the marriage rather than months. This is especially true for spouses serving in the Reserves.

The three methods used to determine amount of payment in the United States of America are:

- Net Present Value - This is more common if someone wants a buyout up front. The former spouse can be awarded a specific dollar amount or percentage of the present value of the pension.
- Deferred Distribution - A share amount is calculated at the divorce, but the receipt of funds is deferred until the service member retires.
- Reserve Jurisdiction - This is the most common method. The share the ex-spouse receives is calculated at retirement.

Survivor's Benefit Plan (SBP)

A former spouse can get a share of the pension in the divorce, but if they do not get a share of the SBP, then they will no longer receive pension payments if the service member dies before they do. You can ask that the service member be required to pay into the SBP in order for the ex-spouse to continue receiving pension payments if the service member dies first. Many attorneys have eyes only on the pension division, but the SBP is not a pension. It's a contract for an annuity that replaces the pension if the service member dies.

Service Members Group Life Insurance (SGLI)

Another piece that can be stipulated in a divorce is that in the event that the service member is killed, a certain amount of the policy be paid to the ex-spouse immediately to replace spousal support/child support proceeds, and the remainder be placed in trust funds for any surviving children. Service members would be wise to put an expiration date on this stipulation of the divorce proceedings instead of leaving it open-ended. If the service member's career lasts longer than the children are minors, then he/she may want to designate a new beneficiary once the children are grown.

Military ID Cards

The issue (or question) of ID Cards gets lots of folks into trouble. They mistakenly think that because regulations require them to submit an application for family member ID cards, and because they are listed as the "sponsor," that they can "confiscate" their spouse's ID card any time they choose. Not true - Family member ID cards (and the privilege granted by such cards) are an entitlement, granted by congressional law in the USA, and most likely by other governmental process in other countries. In other words, it's the government who gets to decide who can and cannot have an ID card, not the military "sponsor." A military member who unlawfully takes an military identification card away from his/her spouse can be charged for Larceny under the provisions of Article 121 of the Uniform Code of Military Justice (UCMJ) in the USA. All of the services use the same "joint" regulation which governs the issuance of military identification cards. If the military member refuses to sign the application for an ID for a military dependent, the regulation contains provisions where the Personnel Office may indicate such on the application form, and issue the ID card anyway.

In most cases, the nonmilitary spouse will lose his/her ID card (and privilege) once the divorce is final, with two exceptions (see next page):

- **"20/20/20" Former Spouse** - Full benefits (medical, commissary, base exchange, theater, etc.) are extended to an un-remarried former spouse when:

    ✓ The parties had been married for at least 20 years;
    ✓ The member performed at least 20 years of service creditable for retired pay;
    ✓ There was at least a 20 year overlap of the marriage and the military service.

(Note: If the former spouse is covered by an employer-sponsored health care plan, medical care is not authorized. However, if coverage is terminated, military medical care benefits may be reinstated upon application by the former spouse. They must bring a copy of the divorce decree.

- **"20/20/15" Former Spouse** - The 20/20/15 former spouse qualifies for medical benefits (no commissary, PX, etc.) for one year from the date of the divorce, dissolution or annulment, when:

    ✓ The parties had been married for at least 20 years;
    ✓ The member performed at least 20 years of service creditable for retired pay; and
    ✓ There was at least a 15 year overlap of the marriage and the military service

(Note: If the former spouse is covered by an employer-sponsored health care plan, medical care is usually not authorized, but can be stipulated in the QUADROS documents.)

On the personal side…

Marrying a member of the military has historically been a difficult proposition, no matter the country, culture, or time period. The military member is often away for extended periods of time, and has a rough time adjusting to a normal life when they're back home. Their families have learned to function without them. Unfortunately, divorce is fairly common in the military world.

The military member should be very prepared for accusations of adultery while deployed, PTSD (post traumatic stress syndrome due to battle engagement), arrogance, and a kitchen sink full of other nasty items. Even if the stay at home partner has or had a good support system in the absence of the deployed partner, emotions run high, and small conversational exchanges can turn into something unexpected. Communication is key in any relationship, whether a marriage, a chain of command, or a successful teacher.

Many military members are trained to display arrogance and a sureness of purpose in order to be prepared for battle. That training does not always carry over well into a partnership relationship, and can cause damaging results if used extensively. If you have damaged your relationship as a result of tactics learned in military training, please don't do that again. If you read, try reading this book (or listen to it on an audiobook):

The Five Love Languages

By Gary Chapman

Gary has a lot of other companion books – but the core message is to speak or express love to your mate and family in the language that they understand.

Notes and thoughts:

_____

_____

_____

_____

_____

Divorcing a Passive Aggressive Partner

First of all – what does the term "passive aggressive" mean? Let's take a look at multiple sources to get an idea:

Urban Dictionary: A defense mechanism that allows people who aren't comfortable being openly aggressive to get what they want under the guise of still trying to please others. They want their way, but they also want everyone to still like them.

Wikipedia: Passive-aggressive behavior is the indirect expression of hostility, such as through procrastination, stubbornness, sullenness, or deliberate or repeated failure to accomplish requested tasks for which one is (often explicitly) responsible.

Examples of passive aggressive behavior:

- Giving backhanded compliments – "Wow, I thought that diamond would be bigger" "You look great – if only your hips were smaller…"

- Ignoring your questions – or flat out ignoring you

- Making wistful statements – "I wish I could go" – instead of saying, "Any way I can come?"

- Procrastination – when you ask them to do something, they say they will get to it, and continue whatever it is they are doing – which is often nothing. When asked about it later, they become hostile and aggressive and angry, telling you that they WILL do it if YOU will stop bugging them, but because YOU brought it up again, they WON'T do it.

- Ignoring phone calls

- Leaving someone out of plans – seemingly by accident, but the person being left out feels intentionally slighted. "Forgetting" to tell you about an event so that you miss it.

- Keeping score (tit for tat) – I did this, so you should do that

-

- Blaming – they are never "at fault" – it's always someone else at fault – like YOU. Example – It's not my fault that I didn't come up to visit your mother at the hospital, I was about to come up there but then you asked why I wasn't there and you were snappy with me so I felt un-welcome and wasn't about to come up there, it's YOUR fault I wasn't there…

Does any of this sound familiar to you? If so, writing it down can help you identify and clarify these behaviors:

_____
_____
_____
_____
_____
_____
_____
_____
_____
_____
_____
_____
_____
_____

Passive Aggressive behavior has 100% deniability and 0% accountability. When you decide to divorce a passive aggressive partner, you may have thought that you're finally going to resolve the issue – but you have a different kind of battle ahead of you.

These are some of the tactics that a passive aggressive partner will employ during divorce – now granted, they may actually do these things without thinking – its part of who they are, they just do it naturally.

- They will miss deadlines for document filings and court dates. Plan to spend more time and money than a normal divorce simply because your partner will string things along – and blame you because it's all your fault.

- They will agree to a mediated divorce to save costs, but will then refuse to sit down and negotiate the terms of the divorce with the mediator. They may finally make the mediator appointment, and then quibble over who will pay the mediation fee.

- Prepare for your passive aggressive partner to demand custody of the children – not because they really want custody, but they want to punish YOU and interfere with your relationship with the children. They will also threaten you with regards to the children, telling you that no matter what the court says, you'll never get to see the kids. Don't let their threats bother you – they are just threats.

- If the passive aggressive partner is ordered to pay child support to you, expect a slow leak of voluntary payments until the court ordered payments begin from their wages. In reality – they will probably not make any voluntary payments. Your passive aggressive ex-partner may change jobs with the specific intent of stopping child support payments, and forcing the child support enforcement division to "catch up" with them.

- If your passive aggressive partner is on social media, expect carefully crafted posts that paint your partner as a "martyr" suffering through difficult times. Also expect his or her friends and family to hear tales that you are experiencing a personal crisis, psychological breakdown, delusions, PTSD, or other mental illness.

The best way to "prepare" for the battles and long-term war that will be the divorce and aftermath of splitting from a passive aggressive partner – is just to be aware of these tactics, and recognize them for what they are.

- When there are specific dates pending – call them the night before and morning of the due date. E-mail them. Text them. Be relentless.

-
  - Avoid social media – if at all possible, delete your account for the months before, during, and after the divorce proceedings. Why? Because you have shared friends and family. Your passive aggressive partner's posts will get back to you from other sources, and it's better if those sources come to you verbally for confirmation, rather than filtered to you digitally.

  - **THERE IS NO REASONING WITH YOUR PARTNER**. Just don't even start. There are some things that you have to discuss – do your best to get your point across, and terminate the communication. Your partner will do their best to twist your words and use "guilting" tactics to return to relationship patterns that got them their way in the past – you offering to do something or give them something without them specifically asking for it. Do not continue to fall into this pattern.

Question: People are starting to ask me what's going on, that my partner is accusing me of having a nervous breakdown, PTSD, etc. What do I tell them?

Take the high road (that means to be really nice). There's no need to divulge personal relationship details, or launch into an attack and analysis of your partner's passive aggressive behavior. Simply say – "There are two sides to every story, and you've evidently heard a lot of one side. Divorce is never an easy thing, he/she is just having a difficult time, and I ask you to be supportive of him/her as she works through the process."

Question: My ex keeps forgetting to tell me about the kid's school programs, and I always miss them. How can I make them tell me?

You can't make them tell you. Call the school, tell them that you're not getting copied in on your child's activities, and request that you be added as an equal participant for all notifications. Schools are getting savvy to this, and are setting up centralized bulletin boards on websites, and e-mail newsletters. You can also arrange for a weekly call with the teacher if you feel that you need verbal confirmation of your child's school progress.

Question: My partner has stretched out the divorce negotiations for months now, every week there's one more thing to hash out, and then he/she needs the weekend to think about it. How can I speed up the process?

You really can't – if you want to negotiate. If you are done with negotiations, and you have given them more than enough chances – you can take the "apocalyptic" or "nuclear" approach. Take them to court and let the judge decide. For some people, if they have given absolutely everything that they can afford to give in the negotiations yet their passive aggressive partner is still bargaining for more – court can be a viable option that actually gives you a better deal. You've tried to be nice – yet your partner is being unreasonable. Let the judge have a go at it. It will cost both of you – but it can also put an end to the game-playing.

Notes and Thoughts:

CHAPTER THIRTEEN

Divorcing a Narcissistic Partner

What does it mean to have a narcissistic partner? You may have been courted early on with sweet words and promises, lured in by a very charming person. But after a while, you begin to feel that something's not quite right. Your life revolves around your partner, they've driven away all of your friends and family, and are extremely critical of you and your actions.

Narcissism is a personality disorder (NPD – Narcissistic Personality Disorder), and there is a spectrum inside the disorder. Your partner may be mildly narcissistic, all the way up to full-blown narcissism. If your partner is on the mild side, you can have a better outcome with a good attorney, a mediator to structure the settlement, and even some counseling or psychological/psychiatric help.

A full-blown NPD may even be "gas-lighting" you, making you feel like you're worthless, that you can't make a decision without their guidance. You need to recognize what's happening to you, and stop your reaction. You are a complete person, you can make decisions, you are an adult. Act like one!

When you decide to divorce, you will be threatened by your partner:

- I'll fight you with every cent I have!
- You'll be living on the streets when I'm finished with you!
- You'll never see the kids again!
- You won't survive without me!

If any of these phrases have come out – you may be fighting with a narcissistic partner. Unfortunately – these may not be idle threats from them. Before you ever start the divorce, you need to be prepared to fight.

Start a written journal – When your partner criticizes you or acts out – write it down. This can establish a pattern of narcissistic abuse that you can present to your attorney, and the court.

Get all of the financial information you can before you drop the divorce bomb – If your partner has control of the finances, you need to run a credit report on yourself, your partner, and both of you as a couple. Get a copy of your last tax return, up to three years if possible (www.irs.gov – you can request one). The credit report and tax return will give you a better idea of what's going on, especially if there are assets that you don't know about, or that your partner is hiding from taxation.

Get a lawyer that is familiar with the personality disorder – Once you describe your partner's behavior, a good attorney should know what to do. They may recommend a Temporary Restraining Order (TRO) if your partner becomes abusive – and they may recommend additional cautions. Follow their advice.

Make sure everything is in writing – Any promises and agreements should be in writing. Ask that your partner either text or e-mail you. If they are verbally threatening, insist that they contact you only by e-mail. That way you have a record of their behavior towards you.

Keep it away from the kids – NPD partners will use your children as a tool against you, because they know that the children are important to you. Be sure to keep a written account of any accusations that your partner throws your way – they'll call you a bad parent, they may try to turn your friends and family against you (if they haven't done it already). Write it down. If they try to start a fight with you in front of the children, walk away from it. Do not engage.

CHAPTER FOURTEEN

When the Crazy Goes Down

Crazy Stuff happens in a breakup

You've heard the stories, hopefully you won't be one. But just in case, some things below are just a "heads up, buttercup".

Did Someone Cheat?

If there are allegations of <u>sexual</u> and/or <u>financial</u> infidelity, call all of your shared Financial Institutions immediately. Freeze accounts until everything can be examined (be sure you have enough to live on if there is a dispute). This includes checking and savings accounts, credit unions, credit cards. You might want to get a credit report to see the extent of the damage you may be facing. Hate to tell you - but you are most likely stuck with the aftermath even if the judge deems that all of the debt belongs to your partner. It'll take months to sort it out with creditors and credit bureaus. Whether a partner has been spending community money on a third-party personal relationship, or a bad business relationship, put a stop to it.

In many states, allegations of adultery do not matter in the legal proceedings, it still may go down as "Irreconcilable Differences". It may be best for all to just go your separate ways and <u>not</u> announce to everyone in a public forum that there was bad behavior. Mudslinging leaves everyone dirty. If you are truly into the whole prosecution thing, some states have provision for "Alienation of Affection" and will allow you to sue the interfering party that your partner took up with (which, if the home-wrecker is a woman, you may be calling "THE HO", and if you are a guy, you may call him...hmmmm...what do you call him – I'm thinking "Gigolo", maybe?)

Were you cheated on? Feel like venting? Do it. Right here. Right now.

_____

_____

_____

_____

_____

Is Your Ex-Partner (or Soon-to-be-Ex) Stalking You?

If your partner is stalking you in any way, you need to be very clear to them that their behavior is unacceptable, and that you will not tolerate it. Examples of stalking behavior are:

- **Excessive phone calls**
- **Excessive texts or IM's via computer or chat service**
- **Excessive e-mails, copying e-mails to both personal and work accounts (especially if you are ignoring them)**
- **Showing up at your work or home unannounced** - they need to call, text, or e-mail first, and their visit needs to be accepted and for a definite reason, and then they need to leave. Appearances by your ex (or soon-to-be ex) are not welcome, and they need to understand that you do not want to talk it out anymore, you are done. And don't YOU be the one stalking if your ex, or soon-to-be-ex, is the victim. And yes, you could be victimizing them if they do not wish to see you or talk with you.
- **Making comments about you on social media** - If your ex is making comments about you on Facebook / Twitter / Instagram / Snapchat / etc. in such a way that it is sure to get back to you, that is stalking as well. Even if it's saying really nice things about you behind your back - that is a "guilting" tactic, trying to make you into the bad guy to pressure your friends to convince you to take them back. That is stalking, and it is unwelcome, and you need to make it clear that they need to stop. Consider deleting your social media account(s) for a few months to escape the noise.
- **Saying or writing nasty and/or untrue things about you** – Yes, it's a nuisance. But unless the issue is causing you undue financial hardship, ignore it. If the problem is causing financial and other negative implications in your life, and you can prove and document their behavior, get with your attorney and file a slander (for verbal attacks) or libel (for written attacks) lawsuit against your ex (or soon-to-be ex). This may stop the behavior without having to actually go to court – but you may need to actually go through with the case if you wish to recover damages against them.
- **Giving unwanted gifts** - Your ex may initiate a courting behavior trying to "win" you back. Do not accept gifts, return them immediately. If it is perishable items, such as food or flowers, give them away, and let them know that you gave them away.
- **Using Threats or Actual Violence to Gain the Upper Hand** - Some people will use threats of physical violence, financial devastation, or deprivation of access to the children in an attempt to force their partner to do something. Be firm, and be clear, that this type of threat is unacceptable. Report this immediately to your legal professional, there may be legal/judicial steps to be taken to prevent escalation. In some cases, police protection may assist in quelling the problem. But in some - you may have to take some type of drastic action - in any case, seek professional help to secure your safety, and that of your children.
- Making any type of written or verbal or implied threat in any fashion - "If you don't take me back, you'll be sorry." "You'll never see your kids again if you leave." "You are worthless, you'll never survive without me to take care of you." (If they're saying the last one to you - **you are being abused,** and your abuser is cruel and obnoxious.)

-
- Performing violence to you or your personal property
- Threatening your job, your family, your friends

In any of these cases - you MUST tell someone. In most cases, Law Enforcement officials cannot help you until the threat is carried out. Seek legal help, and try to get a restraining order or some other type of legal instrument filed to make any further behavior punishable by law enforcement officials. There are special security firms that you can hire to provide personal protection against threats of this nature – unfortunately, they are usually pretty expensive. You may need to resort to carrying some type of a weapon to defend yourself, if your ex-partner becomes physically violent. Check the regional laws in your area in regards to personal weapons, some may not be legally acceptable to carry. Be smart, but also be safe.

Be prepared – do you have a place to go if you need to "disappear" for a while? Someplace that your partner doesn't know about, someplace that your friends won't tell where you are?

_____

_____

_____

_____

_____

_____

_____

_____

Don't Take Their Word For It

Get everything in writing, everything. You may also have to stoop to secretly audio or video-taping, depending on your situation. If the relationship with your partner is extremely broken, insist that they either 1) make all requests by e-mail so that you have written proof of their requests and your responses, or 2) insist that all communications go through your attorney. Number two will cost you, just saying. Your attorney will most likely bill by the quarter hour, and even in a small town they'll charge $250 an hour USD.

If Violence is Involved – Get Out Now

If you are being abused in any way, or even threatened, leave the home that you have shared with your abusive partner. Find a safe place – and keep in mind that a safe place may not be with your parents or your friends. You may need to seek anonymous shelter – evaluate all of your options.

Wrap Your Head Around It

If you have any mental reservations about the proceedings (maybe you are the partner that has been filed on), it is in your best interest to talk to someone about what's going on. That does NOT mean to talk smack about your soon-to-be-ex to everyone you know - this means talking to your priest, rabbi, psychiatrist or counselor about what's going on. Splitting up a household is a big life event, and filled with emotions. Having someone to talk with you about what's going on can help smooth the psychological impact of the event.

You may also need medical assistance if the process is causing you to have depression or anxiety. Don't be shy, but don't get addicted to mind-numbing drugs, either.

Some people cope by exercising, practicing yoga, meditation, or other physical exertion. Find what keeps you centered, and stay with it.

What is, or will be, your coping mechanism, your "feel good" practice to get over your divorce?

_____

_____

_____

_____

_____

_____

_____

Helping Your Partner Cope

If your partner is not coping well, try to get them to help themselves. You are not their parent, even though you may have acted as a parent in the past.

- Give them a list of contacts to call, and let them make the call – lawyers (not yours), realtors or apartment properties, utilities, etc.

- Be considerate of their grieving - they loved you (or your attention, your money, your social status, etc.)

- Don't let them threaten you into doing what they want in regards to the split up - they may threaten to harm themselves, to harm you, or to harm your children or your family if you do not comply with their wishes. (Refer to Chapter 11 – Divorcing a Passive Aggressive Partner, and Chapter 12 – Divorcing a Narcissistic Partner)

- Don't buy into their threats, get help from law enforcement, get help from a psychiatric professional. If you are still married – you can have them committed to a mental institution for 30 days (in many regions).

- If it comes down to it - again, insist that all communication be by e-mail or text so that you have documentation of their hurtful, abusive or threatening words.

- If necessary, keep a diary or journal of your partner's actions to establish mood and motive. This is not to be vindictive to your partner - it is protecting your own interests, and those of your children.

What things will you do, or STOP doing, to help your partner separate from the relationship?

_____

_____

_____

_____

_____

_____

Don't Be That Person...

Once the legal proceedings are over - don't be that person that goes back to your ex for one more afternoon of fun. Just don't. Move on.

Is It Worth Saving?

Well, is it? If it is, then by all means - try to save it. (Refer to **Chapter One – Do you REALLY want to break up / divorce?** in this book!) But don't do it alone, do it WITH your partner (and if they don't want to attend, think about that – is it really worth saving?). Attend counseling. Attend marriage workshops and classes. Identify what is wrong, how it got wrong, and BOTH of you have to work towards fixing it. Marriage is NOT a 50/50 proposition, it's 100% on both sides. If both of you are not committed, then take a pass and move on. If BOTH of you want to salvage it - **avoid the following scenarios:**

- **Religious-based counseling** - Sometimes this may help, if you are BOTH committed to your faith. But if just one of you is committed to the faith, the other will find this type of counseling to be a painful and excruciating exercise in idiocy. Try a different route for better results.
- **Counseling where the counselor does NOT ask to speak with you individually** (He Said and She Said sessions - forgive the gender references in this case, it is meant as an example, not to imply that the relationship would be male/female necessarily) then brings you together for couples counseling. When you have a counselor that tries to work things out with just the couple together - you, or your partner, will most likely hold back some crucial information that the counselor needs to know to decide if the relationship really can work. Ask for the separate sessions so you can air your beefs, and let your partner air their beefs as well, and THEN get back together with the counselor.
- **Letting a friend or family member handle your counseling** - Not cool. They may know you, they may have the credentials to do the counseling, but it is a conflict of interest for them to take your case.

Question: My religion is going to ex-communicate me if I leave my spouse or get a divorce.

If you are very religious, this is a huge decision for you. You may lose your support community, friends, family, neighbors, if you choose to make this decision. If that is your entire identity, you may need to think a lot before choosing this path. If your life is in danger from your spouse or your community, you need to escape the situation as quickly as possible and find a shelter to assist you as you transition into a new society, and possibly a new identity.

One thing to keep in mind – ex-communication is a people-process, decided by people, not your spiritual power. Are you going to be ex-communicated from a social group, or cut off from your spiritual power? Your spiritual power is not held by people, it's held by a higher power. Your higher power will not cut you off because of what other people say or think.

Question: My ex has custody of the kids – and won't let me talk to them or see them. What can I do to make my ex comply with the court orders for visitation?

Unfortunately – not much. The police won't do anything. You can take them to court – but the judge will just frown at them, slap their hand and tell them to do better. Our current judicial system falls very short of "making" people do the things that they are supposed to do when they are grown ups. Read the next question and answer for more information.

Question: My ex has custody of the kids – and the kids keep telling me that they're not getting fed, they're being fed junk food all the time, and that my ex is never there to take care of them, they're failing out of school, what can I do?

Again – there's not a lot you can do – unless you want to go back to court and fight for custody of your children. In order to be successful at this project – you need to have the following ducks in a row:

- Keep a diary or journal of your observations of how the children have been mistreated by your ex.
- Get your child's school records to demonstrate how their grades have fallen while in your ex's custody since you don't have day to day influence on their activities
- Make sure all of your communications with your ex are by e-mail – print out copies if there is evidence that your ex has contradictory or questionable behavior with regards to the child or children.
- Get a really good attorney that is willing to assist you. Prepare to pay them a minimum of $15,000 if your ex decides to fight you.
- If you are currently NOT married – you might want to consider GETTING married to show a stable home life (but ONLY if you are in a committed relationship that is worthy of a marital bond – you've been there before, don't make another mistake!)
- Worst case – have social services pay a visit to your children's home. If they get involved, there is a better chance that your ex may get the message that they need to work harder at this child-raising thing. If it's really bad – they can take the children out of the home. Be aware that <u>they may not even notify you if that happens</u>. The children may be taken into protective custody and put into foster care without your consent. <u>You MUST keep tabs on them AT ALL TIMES if you go this route</u>, or if you find out that social services is interested in their home life. If conditions are as bad as you think they are – this may be a quicker way to obtain custody of the children without a long and drawn-out court fight. Unless your ex tries to get them back through the social services and court process – then, yes, be prepared to fight.

What things are you questioning, or are afraid of with your divorce?

CHAPTER FIFTEEN

Miss Manners

Breaking up in the 21st Century

We all remember Miss Manners and Emily Post - or we've at least heard of them Let's have some discussion on being nice about the break-up.

Facebook - What's appropriate?

- **Status** - When you are separated, you can keep your "In a Relationship" status if you choose. You can also change it to "It's Complicated". It's not appropriate to change to "Single" until you are legally declared single, if you were legally married before. In my divorce, we left our statuses as married throughout the divorce process, until the very end. When I changed mine to "Single", my ex was very offended, and un-friended me. Which was really for the best as time went on, it was an important lesson for me.
- **Friend Status with your Ex** - If there were/are some bad feelings, chances are you have already "un-friended" each other. If not - you really should. Studies have shown that ex-partners that stay friends on Facebook have difficulties moving on from the relationship, and suffer un-necessarily by seeing daily activities of their ex-partner. Now - years down the road, it may be okay to re-friend your ex. As in many years. As in five or more. Things to consider - if you initiated the divorce, they may think that you accepting their friend request may think that you would be amenable to a reconciliation. It is better to ignore a re-friend request, or send a nice e-mail with a "thanks, but I like to keep my life private" message. They are no longer a part of your life, even if you share children.
- **Announcement?** - It's really not necessary to make an announcement about your relationship status. Everyone figures it out.

Have you changed your Facebook status? ❑ Yes   ❑ No   ❑ Not Yet

Have you un-friended your partner/ex-partner? ❑ Yes   ❑ No   ❑ Not Yet

Why, or why not?

_____

_____

_____

Instagram / Twitter / Snapchat / Tumblr / Periscope (etc.)

1. Don't follow your Ex - that's called stalking.
2. Block them from following you - prevent stalking.

Have you un-followed your partner/ex-partner? ☐ Yes ☐ No ☐ Not Yet

Have you blocked your partner/ex-partner? ☐ Yes ☐ No ☐ Not Yet

Why, or why not?

_____

_____

_____

_____

Printed Announcements

Some enterprising companies have started marketing printed announcements, similar to engagement announcements, wedding or birth announcements. Divorce/Break-up announcements are just tacky. Don't. It's not like you're registered at Macy's or Target.

Break-Up Celebrations

Okay - now this could be a cathartic event with a few close friends. Las Vegas is even marketing these events to the newly single. Just don't be too crazy - alright, do what you need to do. Just have a designated... driver / chaperone to make sure you don't do something really stupid - like wind up married again...

Are you planning a break-up celebration? If so, what will you do, who will you celebrate with?

_____

_____

Break-Up Jewelry

This idea has been around for a long time. Taking some of the jewelry that the ex gifted you with and having it turned into something new, something different. Take that bling ring / necklace / bracelet and make it into a new piece. Nothing wrong with that.

Do you have jewelry from your marriage that you want to make into something new? What will you do?

_____

_____

_____

Have you thought about giving your jewelry to other family members, or selling the jewelry? Selling the jewelry can help you pay expenses for everyday living, or to do something special. You could also donate the proceeds to a charity. Something to think about!

The Name Game

For the ladies - many may have changed their last name when they married. When divorcing - what name to take? Things to consider:

- **If you have young children** - taking back a maiden or previous last name can be confusing to the children and their social/education system. But with the proliferation of children staying with remarried mothers that take a new husband's last name, this is more and more common.
- **Confusion with new wife** - If the former husband remarries and you keep his last name, you may be confused with her at social and educational events. This can be extremely embarrassing both for you, and for her. I know a woman that has been divorced for over 20 years, but kept her married name, and still insists that she is his legal and faithful wife according to the laws of the church she was married in. She even successfully fought the church annulment after the legal divorce had been complete for over 10 years. Behavior like that is really vindictive and childish – move on. Other childish behavior is keeping your former husband's name just to make him mad and remind him of whatever. Don't.
- **Career branding** - If you have degrees and a professional career built with your married last name, it may be difficult to keep that branded prestige if you change your last name.
- **Separate identity** - Sometimes you just want to establish yourself as separate and distinct from who you were when you were married to that person, and a change is in order.

As you can see, this is a complicated decision. Keep in mind that some courts charge a name changing fee, it may be cheap, it may be over $100, but most regions allow the name change as part of the Dissolution Agreement.

CHAPTER SIXTEEN

Things I Wish I'd Known

Here are some things that you may learn along the way - but you get to learn them in advance and know them ahead of time!

1) **Your attorney/legal professional may friendly - but they are not your friend**. They are trying to make money, and when they sit and listen to all of your problems for half an hour - they will charge you for that time. At double or triple the rate of your counselor. Probably just double what your psychiatrist charges. Keep that in mind. It's much cheaper to call a friend, or vent on the subway to a stranger. (Don't vent on Facebook. Just don't.)

Are you calling your attorney a lot? Are they running up your legal bill by listening? Can someone else listen to you and help solve the issue differently, rather than with legal means?

_____

_____

_____

2) **Your break-up may start out amicable, but by the time it comes time to sign papers, your partner may have turned into a nasty, snotty shrew**. If you are the initiating party - don't back down and apologize for breaking up. If your partner has filed on you and they are nasty because you have fought the proceedings, don't apologize for fighting. It's okay to fight for certain things - but fighting to keep a sinking ship afloat is usually a lost cause. Find a life boat, and gracefully depart.

Got bad feelings about how it's going? Write them down. Vent. It's okay to acknowledge your emotions, you don't have to hide them.

_____

_____

_____

3) **It may take a long time to recover**. Even if you are the one that initiated the process, you may find yourself still harping on it a couple of years later. Consider getting therapy to help overcome your anger and sadness about the failed relationship.

Do you think that counseling or therapy might help you get over your divorce aftermath? Why, or why not?

_____

_____

_____

_____

_____

_____

4) **Trying to hurt your ex usually backfires**. Letting everyone know that he/she had an affair may satisfy your need for revenge - but your ex could lose their job, and then you and your children could lose alimony and child support and health care. If you are still in the separation proceedings, the loss of income could eat up all of the shared assets and you could be left penniless. Moving forward – you WILL have to see your ex at weddings, funerals, etc. Do you really want them to be forever angry with you? Be wise, and don't play the revenge game.

Do you want revenge against your ex? It's normal. If you could, what would you do? Write it down – and then let it go.

_____

_____

_____

_____

_____

5) **Being divorced/split-up doesn't mean you are less competent, a failure, or less desirable**. It just means your relationship didn't work out. You may be in a social group or culture that frowns upon the split-up - seek other company for friendship and social interaction. Move on.

What are you going to do to regain or rekindle your own self-esteem that may have been damaged by your relationship?

_____

_____

_____

_____

_____

_____

_____

_____

6) **You may lose some friends. If you shared friends as a couple, they may choose sides**. If they did - they weren't really your friends to begin with. You will make new friends.

What friends do you think you might lose? Why will you lose them?

_____

_____

_____

7) **You may never be "friends" with your ex.** You may agree to be "friends" when you start the break-up process...but it may not work out. Let it go, but be civil if you have children together.

What is your vision for your relationship with your ex in the future? Is it realistic? How will/can you cultivate this vision?

_____

_____

_____

_____

_____

_____

8) **You might stay in touch with some of your ex's family.** This can go either way, you just never know. You may see them because of shared children, and they will shoot you the stink eye. Or – they may have always liked you as a person, and they'll still remain friendly towards you after the divorce. Don't be surprised either way.

Will you miss your ex-partner's family? Who will you miss the most? Who are you glad to let go of?

_____

_____

_____

_____

_____

_____

9) **No matter how bad things were, you will miss your ex at some point.** You may miss talking to them about something. Don't be tempted to call them up. That relationship had an expiration date, and it's expired.

Do you think you'll miss your ex-partner? Why or why not?

_____

_____

_____

_____

_____

_____

10) **You will not be alone forever.** Seriously. But...if you've let yourself go - fix that. Lose it, gain it, color it, slap some makeup on it, dress it up. Ask a friend to take you shopping and help makeover your wardrobe (Goodwill has some good stuff, don't be shy if you're broke!). Try some new colors, some new styles. Try a new hairstyle

Are you afraid of being alone? Why or why not?

_____

_____

_____

_____

_____

11) **Divorce/Splitting-Up can be the beginning of A New You**. This is your chance to begin again. Whether your relationship was four months or forty years - you are worthy as an individual. You have value to yourself, and society as a whole. Make a new healthy habit - make several. Make a change in your appearance. Be someone different - because you are.

It's okay to be single, it's okay to be "alone" and not be in a relationship. You do not need to start dating right away, or ever. You may decide that being single is what you always wanted, and it gives you peace to devote your time and efforts to – YOU.

If you do start dating, be careful. Be mindful. Don't date just to date, unless you are just looking for companionship and not anything permanent. Let your dating partners know your expectations up front.

- If you are dating with the intent to marry, let them know up front your mindset.
- If you are looking for a strictly physical relationship, let them know.
- If you are looking for a strictly spiritual or platonic relationship with no physical intimacy, let them know.
- If you have any health issues, let them know. Don't hide things from potential partners, unless there is a very good reason. That may be why you're not married anymore – don't repeat past mistakes.

What are your plans for your new life?

_____

_____

_____

_____

_____

_____

_____

_____

CHAPTER SEVENTEEN

After the Divorce Checklist

Living Alone/Apart

- ❑ Make a new friend. Do something with a friend or friends every week.

- ❑ Get outside – breathe fresh air. Even if the weather isn't great.

- ❑ Take a class – learn something new. Udemy.com offers courses free and cheap, and you can take a lesson in as little as two minutes. Take one lesson a day – or more!

- ❑ Read new books – if you read. Try a different author, or a different genre.

- ❑ Find new music. Check out the trending tunes on iTunes.

- ❑ _____

- ❑ _____

- ❑ _____

- ❑ _____

Financial

- ❑ Make your budget – and stick to it

- ❑ If you receive a cash settlement – don't spend it all. Bank it in savings, invest it in an IRA or stable stocks. If there are outstanding debts with unreasonable interest rates, pay them off.

- ❑ Finalize sale of house, other assets.

- ❑ If you receive part of your partner's 401(k), be sure to go through the steps to roll it into your own account – don't spend it. If the distribution is mis-handled and you DO end up paying taxes on it, go ahead and buy an IRA with the remainder (consult a CPA). You may be able to use the cash at year end to buy into your own existing 401(k) if you did not hit the maximum contribution through payroll deduction.

- ❏ Change name with picture ID if applicable. Also change with Social Security Administration / other governmental agency. They usually like to see the original copy of the divorce decree, and evidence that you intend to use a different name – like a receipt that you've applied for a new state issued picture ID. You may want to go ahead and get a new passport at this time.

- ❏ Establish new credit card(s). If your credit is shot – don't worry, someone will issue you a card. You want to find a lender with a "secured" program. What you do is establish a savings account with their institution, and they issue a credit card with a line of credit equal to the savings account. As you use the card and make regular payments, they usually extend the line of credit without requiring additional deposits to the savings account. This allows you to establish, or reestablish a credit history.

- ❏ _____

- ❏ _____

- ❏ _____

- ❏ _____

Children

- ❏ Establish visitation schedule. The court will typically offer a standard every Wednesday night from 5pm to 9pm and alternating weekends schedule. This may not work with your schedule or your children's activities. Try to be civil and flexible.

- ❏ Establish holiday schedule. Again, the court will offer alternating holidays on odd and even years. This may cause issues with extended family plans, try to be civil and flexible.

- ❏ Establish pickups/meetings. If phone calls are acceptable – answer the phone. If not, read your texts. Don't be late, be courteous – and civil and flexible.

- ❏ Offer/obtain counseling for your child or children if necessary.

- ❏ Buy/read them helpful books.

- ❏ Make new traditions and find new activities to do with your kids that you did not do with your partner. Make new memories. Show them love.

- ❏ Do not smack-talk your ex in front of your kids (important!)

❑ _____
❑ _____
❑ _____
❑ _____
❑ _____

Closing Remarks

Divorces and Break-ups aren't fun. They are emotional roller coasters, financial merry go rounds, and no one really wants to be on these un-amusing rides. Make the best of it, plan carefully, hope for the best, and expect the worst.

Please be sure and use the **Assets & Debts Spreadsheet** from the program – please visit www.dragongempublishing.com/flaunchyourdivorce to get a copy. I would appreciate your feedback as to how I can improve the book, the checklists, spreadsheet, and the book resources that I've listed.

Please keep in mind that this is a generic book that is not going into specific details about each country or state that grants divorces. There is some specific information about the USA military mentioned, but most militaries in the world follow similar legal codes. If you feel that it's important that specific information be added to the book to make it more valuable for all users, please, contact me at:

wanda@dragongempublishing.com

Also, if you would like to join my mailing list for updates and information on future books and courses, please sign up on the website.

Thank you so much for going through the Launch Your Divorce workbook, I hope that your divorce or split-up has a better blueprint for success with the points that you've learned, and can take away and share with your friends and family.

"I am not what happened to me. I am what I choose to become."

~ Carl Jung

Appendix A - The Divorce Playlist

These are tunes for all ages. Party it up, sit down and cry – they're all here. Gather some friends, or gather some Kleenex. If you go to my webpage (www.dragongempublishing.com/launchyourdivorce) I've setup links to the songs if you'd like to listen/buy…

You Oughta Know – Alanis Morisette
According To You – Orianthi
All My Ex's Live in Texas – George Strait
Already Gone – Kelly Clarkson
Black Coffee in Bed – Squeeze
Careless Whispers – Wham
The Crying Game – Boy George
Done – The Band Perry
The End of the Innocence – Don Henley
Fast Car – Tracy Chapman
Forget You – Cee Lo Green
Habits (Stay High) – Tove Lo (don't be her)
You Don't Bring Me Flowers – Neil Diamond/Barbara Streisand
I Fall to Pieces – Patsy Cline
I Keep Forgettin' – Michael McDonald
I Know There's Something Going On – Frida
I Wanna Be Around – Tony Bennett
I'm Not the Only One – Sam Smith (don't be him, either)
In The End – Linkin Park
Leave (Get Out) – JoJo
I Can't Make You Love Me – Bonnie Raitt
The Power of Goodbye – Madonna
Prayer in C – Lilly Wood
Rolling in the Deep – Adele
Say Something – A Great Big World w/Christina Aguilera
Send in The Clowns – Judy Collins, also by Frank Sinatra, Barbra Streisand…
She's Got You – Patsy Cline
Since U Been Gone – Kelly Clarkson
Someone Like You – Adele
When I Was Your Man – Bruno Mars
Tonight I Wanna Cry – Keith Urban
You'll Think of Me – Keith Urban
Tracks of My Tears – Linda Rondstadt, also Smokey Robinson & The Miracles
Someone Like You – Adele
Stronger – Kelly Clarkson
Tainted Love/Where Did Our Love Go – Soft Cell

We Are Never Getting Back Together – Taylor Swift
What A Fool Believes – The Dooby Brothers
Where I Stood – Missy Higgins
Wide Awake – Katy Perry
Wise Up – Aimee Mann
Broken Strings – James Morrison/Nelly Furtado
Dreaming With A Broken Heart – John Mayer
No More I Love You's – Annie Lennox
I Will Survive – Gloria Gaynor
Keep It To Yourself – Kacey Musgraves
Hit The Road Jack – Ray Charles
It's Too Late – Carole King
Un-Break My Heart – Toni Braxton
Before He Cheats – Carrie Underwood
Rootless – Damien Rice
Cry Me A River – Justin Timberlake
On My Own – Patti LaBelle & Michael McDonald
Ain't No Sunshine – Bill Withers
Total Eclipse of the Heart – Bonnie Tyler
Linger – The Cranberries
It Must Have Been Love – Roxette
Screaming Infidelities – Dashboard Confessional
Here's A Quarter – Travis Tritt
Last Love Song – ZZ Ward
Separate Ways – Journey
Part of Me – Katy Perry
Blow Me – Pink
Love Stinks – J. Geils Band
The Scientist – Coldplay
Back to Black – Amy Winehouse
Everybody Hurts – R.E.M.
Love the Way You Lie – Eminem with Rihanna
Nothing Compares to U – Sinead O'Connor
I Heard It Through the Grapevine – Marvin Gaye
Apologize – Timbaland
Somebody That I Used To Know – Gotye
Wrecking Ball – Miley Cyrus
Torn – Natalie Imbruglia
Always On My Mind – Willie Nelson
Crying – k.d.lang with Roy Orbison
Walk On By – Dionne Warwick
Blame Game – Kanye West w/John Legend

You've Lost That Lovin' Feeling – Righteous Brothers
These Boots Are Made for Walkin' – Nancy Sinatra
Take a Bow (Say Goodbye) - Madonna

Add your own songs:

Appendix B – Make Your Own Calendar

If you're not using a calendar app on your phone or computer – you can make your own right here. Fill in the month and days.

MONTH						
Sunday	Monday	Tuesday	Wednesday	Thursday	Friday	Saturday

Event Date   Description

MONTH						
Sunday	Monday	Tuesday	Wednesday	Thursday	Friday	Saturday

Event Date   Description

MONTH						
Sunday	Monday	Tuesday	Wednesday	Thursday	Friday	Saturday

Event Date   Description

MONTH						
Sunday	Monday	Tuesday	Wednesday	Thursday	Friday	Saturday

Event Date   Description

MONTH						
Sunday	Monday	Tuesday	Wednesday	Thursday	Friday	Saturday

Event Date   Description

MONTH						
Sunday	Monday	Tuesday	Wednesday	Thursday	Friday	Saturday

Event Date   Description

MONTH						
Sunday	Monday	Tuesday	Wednesday	Thursday	Friday	Saturday

Event Date   Description

MONTH						
Sunday	Monday	Tuesday	Wednesday	Thursday	Friday	Saturday

Event Date

Description

MONTH						
Sunday	Monday	Tuesday	Wednesday	Thursday	Friday	Saturday

Event Date   Description

MONTH						
Sunday	Monday	Tuesday	Wednesday	Thursday	Friday	Saturday

Event Date   Description

MONTH						
Sunday	Monday	Tuesday	Wednesday	Thursday	Friday	Saturday

Event Date Description

MONTH						
Sunday	Monday	Tuesday	Wednesday	Thursday	Friday	Saturday

Event Date   Description

Do You Want To Write A Book?

Everyone has a book in them – are you ready to publish it? Please visit www.dragongempublishing.com for some help. We offer self-publishing information, and done-for-you publishing packages.

www.ingramcontent.com/pod-product-compliance
Lightning Source LLC
Chambersburg PA
CBHW081946070426
42451CB00017BA/3458